Manager Skills

Complete Step-by-Step Guide on How to Become
an Effective Manager and Own Your Decisions
Without Apology

Improve Yourself Series - Book 6

GARRETT REDFIELD

TABLE OF CONTENTS

INTRODUCTION

If a business is to succeed, it is vital to have not only a manager, but a good manager that can strengthen the employees, expertly communicate, and utilize a range of skills to improve the business as a whole. When a person who does not have managerial skills is promoted to manager, it can only harm the company, and at worst, it will lead to disaster by tearing apart the employees and workflow. Thankfully, good managers are created, not born. While some people do naturally exhibit certain trains belonging to a good manager, they learn these trains through life as they grow. Just as these people have learned throughout their lives to develop managerial skills, you, too, can learn the skills necessary to becoming a good manager. By reading this book and intentionally strengthening your powers of communication, leadership, and empowerment, you, too, can become a first-rate and outstanding manager.

There are many aspects of a good manager, but ultimately they can be refined to six top skills that are a must. These skills include communicating expectations, offering assistance and guidance, encouraging and motivating employees, resolving disputes, empowering employees, and providing objective judgment.

When communicating with expectations, a manager needs to be able to clearly and effectively communicate what is required and expected. This is true not only with employees but also when the manager is communicating needs with the boss or business partners. When there is confusion is only hinders the business, but by learning to communicate clearly and effectively, you can prevent this confusion and ensure everything operates smoothly.

A good manager needs to know when to give their team space to thrive on their own and when to offer guidance and assistance. By learning when to offer suggestions or help in a task, a good manager can help everything run smoothly and effectively, in turn, increasing skill and confidence in the employees.

The end-goal of any manager should be to help their team of employees to reach their full potential. To achieve this goal, a manager should learn how to empower their employees by offering encouragement, training, and opportunities to grow. The manager will openly listen to their employees' suggestions, thoughts, and opinions to help improve the work experience. They will be able to sift through these suggestions to find which are helpful, which can be altered for better results, and which would be unproductive, all the while communicating positivity to their employees so that they feel empowered to continue sharing their thoughts in the future. As the employees feel valued and empowered, it will only improve their work and the workplace.

These are only a few of the managerial skills that

you will learn how to achieve and thrive within the pages of this book. With these skills, you will become the best manager you can be. Even if you are not a manager yet, by learning these skills, you will elevate yourself and become a prime candidate for future managerial positions. All you have to do to succeed is begin reading and applying the information from this book.

If you enjoy this book, please consider reviewing it on Amazon so that others may benefit from it, as well!

CHAPTER 1: RECOGNIZING TALENT AND SURROUNDING YOURSELF WITH A GOOD TEAM

Every manager understands the basics of the hiring process, which involves reviewing job applications, testing potential candidates, interviewing candidates, performing background and reference checks, selecting the best person for the job, and offering the position. However, while these steps are straightforward and easy to understand, there is more that goes on behind the scenes that a successful manager needs to understand. In this chapter, you will learn how to go beyond the basics of the hiring process to recognize talent in individuals and create a reliable team in the workforce.

In this chapter, you will learn techniques that use vital principles for hiring the right candidates. These principles include creativity, challenging candidates, and utilizing your pre-existing team. By using creativity, you can get to better know candidates in-depth by going past the usual questions everyone is prepared to answer. By challenging candidates, you can understand their true talents and abilities, not only seeing who they are on the surface but coming to understand the real person beneath the surface. Lastly, by utilizing pre-existing employees, you can learn how your candidate will interact with your pre-established team and hear the opinions of your staff. Remember, you are not just hiring a single person who will work on an island; you are hiring an individual that will become a part of the team. When you use methods utilizing these three principles, you will find that you can develop the best team. Now, let's look at some techniques you can use to achieve your goals.

Use Innovative Questions

If you stick with the standard interview questions, then you will only ever see the polished surface of a candidate. While these standard questions are undoubtedly important, you also want to throw in some innovative questions as curveballs that will help you to see below the polished surface. This will help you to get a better understanding of the individual, their potential, and their weaknesses. Know that every person will have flaws, but if you understand their potential weaknesses, you can empower the individual and ensure they click with the team.

When asking curveball questions, remember the end-goal: to learn more about your candidate. You could always ask random questions such as "how many tennis balls can you fit in an airplane," as Google's previous senior vice president of people operations,

Laszlo Bock, used to ask. But, Bock ultimately found that random questions such as this are pointless and only serve to make the interviewer feel more intelligent as it does not help you better understand your candidate. Instead, you want your questions to help you learn more about the inner self of a candidate, how they think and operate, how they might interact on a team, and their strengths and weaknesses.

1.If you were an animal, what would you be?

The point of this question is to analyze a person's creativity and self-understanding. You don't even have to ask what animal they would be; you can ask other questions such as *"if you could have any superpower, what would it be?"* or *"if you could have any animal in the world as a pet, what would it be?"* There isn't a single right answer to these questions, as it isn't about what the individual chooses, but rather how they answer. You want their answer to reveal their personality and thought process, rather than being a simple throwaway answer without much thought put into it.

For example, a good answer would be, *"I would be a rabbit because I am usually cheerful and peaceful, but when needed, I can be energetic and hustle to get things done."* Whereas, a bad answer would be *"Probably a cat. Meow."* The correct answer shows the person's thought process and personality, whereas the incorrect answer shows little thought or self-understanding.

Another example, if you were asking about superpowers instead, would be a positive answer of *"I would want the ability to teleport anywhere so that I could travel, visit friends, and get to work all without wasting time or gas."* On the other, an unsatisfactory answer would be, *"I don't know why, but I'd like to fly."* Again, the incorrect answer shows a lack of thought put into the response and little communication. In contrast, with the positive answer, the individual is taking the question seriously, responding with an accurate analysis of themselves, and communicating clearly.

2. Everyone lies at least once on their CV, where is your lie?

While studies have found that as many as one in five job candidates admits to lying on their CV, they won't disclose to this without prompting. You want to understand who this person truly is, and part of that is seeing through potential lies. With this question, you can hopefully catch someone who is a serial offender with lying on their CV, and ultimately find someone who can answer with honesty, confidence, and humor.

A good answer could be, *"It might be a little bit of a stretch saying I "enjoy" staying active, but I do try to stay active even when it's difficult, as I know it's good for my health. But, more seriously, I believe I told the full truth on my CV. I genuinely try to live true to my word, and honestly, as integrity is essential to me."* On the other hand, a bad answers might be a short *"not really,"* *"pass, next question,"* or *"why would you assume I'm lying?!"*

3. Would you rather be liked or feared?

While this may be a character question, it is genuinely a curveball as answering it is not straight forward. You neither want the individual to enthusiastically or offhandedly answer *"feared"* or *"liked."* Instead, you want to see thought put into their answer that goes beyond choosing one or the other, and instead elaborates on the unspoken third answer of balance. After all, you don't want someone who reveals in controlling people through fear, or who allows themselves to be a pushover only so that more people like them.

When answering, you don't want a short answer; instead, the person should elaborate. A response such as *"I don't believe fear is a good motivator, as it leads to an uncomfortable work environment and ultimately causes communication problems. So, I wouldn't want to be feared. And, while I certainly hope people like me, I know it's not always possible. Sometimes you have to make hard decisions to get the job done, and that doesn't always make friends. Because of this, I would much rather be respected and work towards creating healthy relationships with my co-workers with productive communication so that we can work as a team."*

On the other hand, a bad answer would be *"I want to be friends with everyone, I want all of my co-workers to like me," "I want people to fear how much they like me,"* or *"I want people to fear me because if they fear me, I can control the team and get work done."*

4. Where does your boss think you are?

You want an employee that is honest and upstanding. Therefore, this question shouldn't be taken lightly. This means that you don't want an employee that is happy to admit to lying to their boss, even if it's a *"white lie."* However, keep in mind that some bosses are overly controlling and even abusive of their employees. Therefore employees may not be able to be as straightforward as they would like. This is because some bosses might wrongly fire an employee on the spot if they know they are looking for other positions.

An excellent answer to this question would be, *"I prefer to be straightforward and honest, as I am uncomfortable with deception. However, I was able to schedule time off work, and therefore I am doing this in my personal time and saw no need to mention it to my boss at this point. If I get the position, I will then give my boss the standard two week's notice."* On the other hand, an inadequate response would be *"I'm not sure what my boss thinks, I just left on my lunch break, and I don't think my boss will get mad if I'm late to return."*

5. Sell me this pen.

This question is great as it not only helps you see a person's ability to sell a product, but also their general understanding of why a person might buy a pen, what a pen's selling points are, and correctly identifying what you might need. To make this question more challenging, try to use an ugly pen rather than a sleek, expensive pen.

A good answer would be, *"Do you write much in your spare time? What about on the job, do you ever find yourself searching for a pen to write out an important note or schedule? With this pen, you need to look no further. The black ink smoothly glides across the paper, allowing you to write anything you might need effortlessly. The size and shape of the pen are ideal for holding comfortably, whether you are writing for thirty seconds or thirty minutes. With this pen, you can trust that you will always have a reliable writing tool, never being at a loss when you find yourself needing to convey information."* But what would a bad answer be? *"You mentioned earlier that you need a pen, isn't this pen convenient and pretty?"*

Get Away From the Desk and Office

If you are always behind your desk or in your office, you won't get a well-rounded sense of who your candidate is. You want to see how they will act in different environments, watch to see how they might behave when on the job or as part of a team. Keep an eye on how they not only act in the company environment but also how they interact with other people. By merely walking someone through a company workspace, rather than staying in the office, you can better size them up. There are a few main qualities you want to watch for when walking around with a candidate:

1.   Does the candidate treat everyone with respect and as an equal, no matter their position or title?

2.   Is the candidate genuinely interested in the company or organization?

3.   Are they asking questions about the company, employees, management, or how things work?

4.   Is the candidate generally curious?

By walking a candidate through the company, if you pay attention, you can get a firm idea of whether or not they fit in and if you believe they will be a helpful addition to the team. On your walk through the company, be sure to stop and introduce the candidate to a handful of people, so that you can see how they interact and talk.

Along with taking a candidate on a walk through the company, it is also beneficial to leave the company behind and go out to a restaurant for a meal. Of course, if you do this, be sure to ask them about any potential food allergies beforehand, as you would be problematic if you took them to a place that didn't have options without their allergens. For instance, you wouldn't want to take someone with a shellfish allergy to Red Lobster or a wheat allergy to an Italian restaurant. As a manager, you have to be willing to listen to your candidates, and this includes any allergies they might have. If you are unsure of where you can take them to eat safely, ask them where they like to eat!

While taking your candidate out for a meal, you want to watch to see how they handle situations and interact with others. Are they polite, kind, and respectful to the servers? Do they look people in the eye or nervously look away and shift their focus? Will they hold the door and allow others to walk in front, or do they barrel their way through? Can they keep an engaging conversation, ask intelligent questions, and also listen without interrupting? Do they become flustered or angry if there are problems or mistakes? There are many things you can learn about a person by sharing a meal with them, and the importance of taking the time to learn this information about a candidate before hiring them can not be overstated.

Get More Diverse

It is easy to hire a team of people from the same culture and other lifestyle factors as yourself. It is regularly shown that a man is more likely to employ another man for a position, even when there are more qualified women. This is especially true when you consider race, where people of color are less frequently hired and more often discriminated against. But, did you know that by making these mistakes not only are people of color, women, disabled, and other marginalized people harmed, but your company is also losing out on valuable assets?

One great way to ensure your team has the diversity you need is to hire people opposite from yourself purposefully. This means that if you are an able-bodied and middle-aged cis white man, you can try to hire people who are both younger and older than you, cisgender women and trans individuals, LGBTQA+ people, disabled individuals, and people of color. But, what all can these people from different backgrounds and lifestyles offer? At a mere glance, these people can help offer new perspectives, increased creativity, problem-solving, innovation, and more. Let's look at these valuable traits in detail.

1. Creativity

Many businesses thrive off of increased creativity, even when you are not in a traditional "creative" field. Also, if you run a small grocery store, you can still benefit from creativity in all job positions. But, when everyone in your company comes from the same background and circumstances, then everyone will have the same type of creativity. On the other hand, if you celebrate the difference in everyone and have a cultural melting pot of a workplace, you can experience the benefit of creativity that is truly thriving.

2. New Perspectives

Similarly to creativity, when everyone has the same background, then they will have similar skills, experiences, and traits. This can create a stale workplace where progress lags. But, when you engage new perspectives by hiring diversely, you can boost productivity as having a variety of perspectives and experiences will improve planning, strategy, and synergistic teamwork.

3. Innovation

Research by Josh Bersin revealed that when companies are diverse and inclusive, they are 1.7 times more likely to be leaders in innovation, which in turn improves business and profits. This is because when people from a variety of backgrounds and experiences work together, they can come up with brilliant ideas that nobody has put into practice before. Put simply, the more diverse your company, the stronger your company will be on the market. One study conducted across the United States and Europe found that diverse companies are more likely to be top performers when it comes to increased profits.

4. Problem-Solving

A study from the Harvard Business Review found that companies with diverse staff can solve problems more quickly than companies with cognitively-similar teams. By solving problems more quickly, you can resolve potential issues, retain customers, and save money.

5. Reduced Employee Turnover

In many companies, differences can lead to conflict, stress, and eventual employee turnover. But, this frequent stress and turnover only hinders your team and costs your company money. Thankfully, it has been found that when a company is more diverse, people are more likely to be inclusive of differences, therefore increasing positive feelings of acceptance and inner value. As people will feel more secure in their workplace, they will experience increased loyalty to their employer and team, being willing to stick around happily.

6. Improved Reputation

Not only will your employees think better of you if

you maintain a diverse team, but the company's outward reputation with potential customers and clients will improve, as well! At large, people understand that maintaining a diverse workplace is a morally good and socially responsible choice, increasing feelings of positivity and goodwill towards a company that accomplishes this. Your diverse customers and clients will also be happy to see people who resemble themselves in your company, as it will make them feel more valued.

We can all have hidden biases that we are unaware of, as we naturally are drawn to people who remind us of ourselves. For instance, a manager is more likely to hire someone who reminds them of themselves at a younger age, or a "mini-me," rather than someone who is of a different race, religion, and gender. But, by understanding, we all have these biases, and that we can overcome them, we take control and can make better choices. Creating a diverse company begins with making the intentional choice to hire people different from yourself

Get Another Opinion

While it's essential to be able to decide on your own, ultimately, that does not mean you should forgo all outside opinions. After all, a good manager understands the importance of working together with a team of people, and not necessarily doing everything on their own. The same is true through the hiring process. If you discuss potential candidates with someone whose opinion you trust, then they can help confirm or disagree with your perceptions and ideas, ultimately helping you to see a fuller picture of the situation.

Even if you are highly skilled at choosing new teammates for your company, we all make mistakes and have areas we are ignorant to. For instance, while the NFL is skilled at drafting top-notch players, even they make mistakes at times. Tom Brady, who is an incredible quarterback, was only chosen after the sixth round of NFL drafts. People underestimated him, and it affected their ability to see him and his skills. The same can be true of any manager during the hiring process. You can miss out on high-quality talent if you try to go through the process alone. But, if you use your full skill set and all the tools at your disposal, meaning your teammates that you trust, then you can get the most out of the hiring process and end up with the best candidates.

Have Faith in Yourself

If you have followed all of the steps above and still find yourself having doubts about a potential candidate, then it is vital to listen to your gut and understand where these feelings are coming from. One of the most common mistakes that many people make is not listening to their doubts during the hiring process. You might have a nagging suspicion about a person, but not see any evidence to back it up, so you hire them anyway. Before you know it, this person throws off the teamwork in the company, creates drama, rarely shows up on time for work, frequently makes excuses for poor work ethic, and more.

Hiring is a tricky balance, and it takes skill. It is hard to balance between giving a person the benefit of the doubt and ensuring you aren't biased while also listening to your gut and respecting your suspicions. But, if you can manage to balance these aspects, you can hire people who will genuinely benefit your team. When you have doubts about potential candidates, try to analyze the situation and find where these suspicions arise more deeply. This can take a deep and personal understanding of yourself as well as experienced in the hiring process. Over time, you will become more skilled at hiring as you learn how to balance the various important aspects.

At the end of the day, it will be the roll of a dice. By utilizing the methods in this chapter, you can increase your chances of getting a good employee, but you can never guarantee things will work out as you hope. Trust your gut, get a second opinion, use wisdom to follow the tips in this chapter, and in time you will build a team that you can be proud of.

CHAPTER 2: YOU ARE THE LEADER, NOT A FOLLOWER

"If your actions inspire others to dream more, learn more, do more and become more, you are a leader." -John Quincy Adams

There are different types of leadership that managers can emulate, and it is crucial to find the method that most fits your personality. For instance, it would be awkward and insincere if you are a more soft-spoken person but attempt to lead in a loud and robust manner. When you try a leadership style that doesn't mesh with your personality, then your team will be able to tell that it is insincere, and you won't be able to inspire confidence. Thankfully, if you understand the various types of leadership that exist, you can find the method that best fits with your personality. When you lead with your natural process, you will be able to not only inspire confidence, but you will also be able to pull up your teammates to a higher level to get the best out of everyone. Now, let's look at the main five types of leadership.

Transformational:

This type of leadership was first defined by scholars and leadership experts Bernard Bass and Bruce Avolio. The transformational leader is incredibly influential, often acting as a role model to those under them. A leader of this type can connect with a team's and individual's sense of identity, and through this process, increase morale and overall job performance. They can transform their entire team by encouraging innovation, creativity, problem-solving, and critical thinking. The transformational leader is often incredibly successful, with some famous ones, including Steve Jobs and Winston Churchill.

Participatory:

A participatory leader understands that everyone in a company or an organization is a team, with their own voice, experience, and strengths. This leader attempts to make use of these unique qualities that everyone possesses with an increasingly democratic, personalized, and hands-on style of leadership. They understand that the team members that will be most affected by a decision should also be involved in the discussions and decision making, rather than bulldozing and ruling them by force. Only by including those who will be affected can you best make use of your team member's strengths.

One great example of the participatory leader is James F. Parker, the former CEO of Southwest Airlines. While post-9/11, most airlines began to cut back on staff, instead Mr. Parker created an innovative profit-sharing program that allowed them to keep their team on hand.

Value-Based:

The leader that focuses on value doesn't encourage their team members with metrics alone but instead chooses to focus on essential core values. By encouraging the team to work towards commonly shared values and goals, the leader can create positive change that fits their organization's mission. This leader does not only claim to have values; they truly act following these values, upholding the principles that the organization is founded on. They can encourage and keep everyone tied together with a common goal for the good of all.

The former president of India, and a well-respected scientist, Dr. APJ Abdul Kalam, is a wonderful example of the value-based leader. His leadership style was so revolutionary that it was used as a model for the Indian Space Research Organization, inspiring the entire company to work together towards commonly shared goals and ethics.

Situational:

The situational leadership style was created as a joint project between behavioral scientist Paul Hersey and bestselling author and business consultant Ken Blanchard. Situational leadership was specifically designed to ideally focus on and target the individual performance needs and behaviors of those that they are leading as a team. A situational leader must have four specific abilities, including:

1.   Understand and diagnose a given individual's ability to complete a particular task in the manner

required.

2. Adapt leadership behaviors based on the situation.

3. Influence and communicate the needed approach for individual teammates that they can fully understand, accept, and act on.

4. Advance the organization by increasing overall performance.

The famed former coach from the NBA, Phil Jackson, is an excellent example of an exemplary situational leader. He was able to successfully manage his entire team and take them to new heights by understanding and utilizing their individual strengths, weaknesses, goals, motivations, and backgrounds.

Servant:

You will often find servant leaders in charitable organizations, as they are naturally drawn to improving those around them. However, a servant leader can excel in any field or organization, whether it is a for-profit company or a charity. Ultimately, a servant leader's goal is to improve both the organization and world at large through equitable and caring leadership. Robert K. Greenleaf first defined this type of leadership as a person who makes an intentional effort to lead by placing the needs of others as the top priority. They fully dedicate themselves to improve the growth of those around them, rather than focusing on themselves.

While it may not sound as if a servant leader could benefit a for-profit company, the opposite is true. Studies have found that when a servant leader leads an organization, it promotes better performance and higher returns. Several examples of servant leaders include Larry Spears, Steven Covey, and Ken Blanchard.

I've written another book on servant leadership, Servant Leadership Skills: Complete Step by Step Guide on How to Learn the Methods to Motivation and Persuasion of individuals (Improve Yourself Series Book 5), so be sure to check that out to learn more on this method!

As there are several types of leadership styles, you might be wondering which is the right choice. The answer is surprising to many people: there is no single "right" choice. All of these leadership styles have their benefits, and what works for you will depend on your personality and team. You might find that you don't strictly fit into a single style, but rather are a combination of two or three methods. You are not boxed in; you can be true to yourself and lead a team to success. While you might see that well-known business people have a different leadership style from you, that doesn't mean you have to copy them. You will do better staying true to yourself and your individual leadership style that fits your strengths rather than trying to copy a manner you find uncomfortable. Instead, you can learn from other leaders in the field and adopt specific methods of theirs while still keeping your unique style.

Being a good leader is about understanding your strengths, weaknesses, and individual style while also remaining agile so that you can deal with any situation in the best manner. You may find that in general, your leadership style is participatory, but at times you might have to use a more servant leadership style when circumstances call for it. The methods you need to utilize will depend on not only your personality and strengths but also your individual team members and the ongoing situation. By understanding yourself and the various leadership styles, you are empowered to adjust your approach based on individual needs, maintaining flexibility and authenticity. This empowerment will increase peoples' faith in you, increasing overall team trust and potential.

However, it is essential to keep in mind that understanding yourself at a deep level and utilizing what you learn to flexibly adjust to any circumstance that comes your way takes hard work, practice, time, and patience. You have to take time to evaluate yourself to understand what inspires you, your values, your weaknesses, and strengths, what you are passionate about, and your aspirations and goals. Once you know these parts of yourself, your primary style of leadership should be apparent, and you may even be able to realize a secondary and third style that you can utilize as the situation requires.

Not only do you need to understand these aspects about yourself, but you need to market them to your team and other people in your organization. Put simply, once you know your strengths, you need to sell these strengths to those around you so that they understand what you have to offer and desire your abilities. For instance, you may display your strengths in listening, communication, and adaptability. As your team members see these strengths in you, they will feel encouraged and empowered as part of the team, pushing them to new heights and increasing the overall effectiveness of the team. Similarly, people in positions above you in the organization will take notice, and it may lead to a promotion or acknowledgment of your services in other ways. Brand and market your strengths, using them to empower those around you, and people will take notice.

While there are several different styles of leadership, all of these styles share some vital skills and qualities at their nucleus. These skills are essential for every leader to learn and develop, as, without these skills, they will be unable to properly lead anyone, much less an entire team of people. Thankfully, you don't have to be born with these skills innately. You can use this book and practice to develop these skills and strengthen them over time.

Skills:
- Inspire Groups of People with a Common Ideal

If everyone is working towards different goals without a shared common ideal, the team will resemble a bunch of scattered puzzle pieces, rather than a single jigsaw puzzle put together with all the parts interconnecting. Find a common ideal that your entire team is motivated by, and inspire people to chase after and follow this ideal.

- Lead by Example

Don't expect your team to act in a way or follow a path that you do not follow. If you are impatient, slow to get the job done, and quick to anger, then you can't expect your team to be patient, ready to accomplish tasks, and slow to anger. Before expecting your team to behave in a given way, make sure that you are leading by example. Follow a path of excellence and high standards, and then your team will follow in your footsteps.

- Remain Flexible and Willing to Take Risk

If you are unwilling to go with the flow, experiment, remain flexible, and take risks, you will be unable to excel. You will be like a rat in a maze that bullheadedly rams into the wall repeatedly, rather than making the needed change in their plan and turning in the other direction. To achieve success, you need to learn when to remain firmly in place, and when to lithely adjust your actions and thoughts to follow a new path.

- Encourage and Empower

Don't only expect people to follow you and then act as if anything less is a failure, and therefore unworthy of praise. This behavior would be as if a child wrote a high-quality, fully-researched, and well-written paper for school, yet only received a "C" as a grade because it's what's expected of them, even though the article is worthy of an "A+" grade. The child will become disheartened over time, as their hard work and effort are never acknowledged, never good enough. When a person follows through with something as expected of them, it is worthy of praise, as they worked hard to accomplish it. Therefore, thank your team and celebrate their accomplishments. Let them know that their effort and handwork are appreciated, and they will continue to give you their best.

- Strengthen the One to Empower the All

Remember that a team is a collection of people, and this collection forms a whole. In this way, a team is both a collection of individual people and a whole group. This is why a team is similar to a jigsaw puzzle, as the puzzle would not exist without each piece. Yet, each piece can not display the entire picture without working and connecting as a whole. If you want to empower your team to be the best as it can be, you have to start with strengthening, building up, and encouraging the individuals that make up the team.

Qualities:

Being a good leader is not only about your leadership style and the skills mentioned above, but your qualities and how you use them to treat others. A good leader must have the skills to connect and interact with others in a way that builds them up, rather than tearing them down.

- Emotional Intelligence

Having a sharp emotional intelligence means that you can understand the emotions of others, the mood of a room, interpersonal dynamics, nonverbal cues, and have empathy. Some people naturally struggle with their emotional intelligence, especially if they are neurodivergent. However, even if you typically struggle with your emotional intelligence, you can proactively work on strengthening it in ways that help you learn to better interact and connect with those around you. Whether you have a naturally high emotional intelligence or have to work to develop it, you can succeed if you understand that these qualities are essential and actively work to build your strengths and overcome your weaknesses.

- Compassion

When a manager doesn't have compassion for their team remembers it is like a slow-acting poison that slowly breaks down the team from the inside out. Many leaders in the business world started out wielding their strengths like a sword, without acting compassionately. But, as they grew and learned, they realized that working in this way only held them back. These business people, such as Jeff Weiner, the CEO of

LinkedIn, learned the importance of working with compassion and made it into a critical aspect of their leadership. By using compassion, Weiner was able to create a team built on understanding, shared values, and trust.

- Vulnerability

Being a leader does not mean that you must appear to be impenetrable and infallible, as we imagine the Ancient Greek gods to be. Even the myths of these great people who were widely respected aren't perfect. Hercules struggled through his tests, and Achilles had his infamously weak heel. Despite these weaknesses, these Greek gods were respected and worshiped. You are not a god, and you won't be revered, but this is a good lesson that nobody is perfect, and we don't need to pretend to be. You can gain more by being honest and vulnerable than you can by putting up a fake whitewashed front. It takes strength to be accurate and vulnerable to embrace the lessons you learn through your failings. But, by embracing these failing and lessons, you can become stronger, wiser, and an overall better leader. People will admire your honesty and vulnerability, and will, in turn, trust you to lead them.

These leadership styles, skills, and qualities are not something most people naturally possess. Even the best business leaders in the world started out making mistakes and having to learn, grow, and develop. These leaders never finish growing; they are continually investing in themselves and building themselves up to be even better business people. Don't expect yourself to know everything and be perfect right out of the starting gate. Give yourself time to invest in your strengths, grow past your weaknesses, and empower your leadership abilities. It takes time to invest in yourself, but it is well worth the rewards you will reap in time.

One way you can invest in yourself is by developing your ability to listen, which is an often overlooked aspect of leadership. There are many ways in which you can strengthen your listening abilities and help your team members to know you are actively listening to them. One of the most potent ways you can do this is with a simple phrase:

"What do you think?"

Sometimes your team members will surprise you, and they might even have better ideas than you do. This is one of the benefits we mentioned previously about hiring diverse staff with different backgrounds and perspectives. They can help you to develop ideas and practices you could not create or come up with on your own. But, asking this only works when you have built a foundation based on listening, and your team trusts that you value their opinion and are genuinely listening and thinking about their words rather than letting it go in one ear and out the other.

To build a foundation of listening, it is essential to know that there are different types of listening, with internal listening, focused listening, and 360 listening being the most important to understand. Let's look at these three listening types.

Internal Listening:

When a person regularly practices internal listening, it reduces feelings of trust and creates fractures in your team's relationships. This type of listening is defined as a person who may be hearing what others are saying, but not focusing and truly deeply listening to the meaning behind their words. With this type of listening, a person is "listening" to their thoughts, values, priorities, and worries while they simply pretend to listen to those around them. Often, people are looking at a smartphone, a computer, papers, or another object while they listen to their thoughts, rather than those around them. We all practice internal listening at times, but it is essential to know that it will cause harm to your team, slowly causing fractures that break apart teamwork and trust.

Focused Listening:

A step towards progress is focused on listening. This type of listening places more focus on the individual talking and is less likely to cause fractures or harm to your team. However, focused listening is still not the ideal method that your team requires to truly build a relationship of trust and understanding that will take your potential to new heights. When practicing focused listening, you aren't looking at your phone, computer, or other distractions. You might even be nodding in agreement as you listen. However, while you hear their words, you are not truly listening to the meaning behind these words and their minute nuances.

360 Listening:

When you practice 360 listening, you begin to build the foundation of trust, value, and truly deep listening that your team requires to flourish. You begin to not only listen to the surface of a person's words, but you are listening deeply to the meaning behind their words, noticing their body language, the tone of their voice, and all the minute nuances. You are fully engaged in the conversation, with no thought of anything else but the present. A deep connection is formed as you truly and deeply listen with your whole heart and soul.

There are a few ways you can proactively develop your 360 listening skills. For example, you can focus on creating more time in your day, looking people in the eye, and asking intentional questions.

If you have every minute of your day scheduled, with no flexibility to listen to your team, then all of your conversations will be rushed. The person you are talking with will sense that you are rushing them, and will, therefore, feel like you don't want to take the time to listen. As if what they have to say is unimportant. Be sure to schedule enough time in your day to truly listen to your team members, not only focusing on what they are saying but genuinely listening to the meaning behind their words as you give them your full attention with 360 listening.

When you look at something while a person is talking, whether your phone or important documents, a person will see that you are not actively listening to them. You are dividing your attention between the conversation and what you are looking at. This not only creates fractures in your relationship with the person as you are not actively listening, but it will also hold you back. You can only fully flourish with your team when you put in the effort to develop your skills, utilize your qualities, and prioritize your listening ability. Put down your phone and papers, close your laptop, and look the person in the eye while you listen.

If one of your team members is asking for advice, be sure that you are truly listening and understanding the situation before you give them an answer. You can do this by asking intentional questions. These questions should clarify what the person needs, and ensure you understand what they intend to communicate. For instance, you might repeat back a variation of what the person said to you. If your team member is struggling to understand how you need something done, you can clarify the situation by asking, "You are struggling to understand how you need to handle this situation, correct?" Once you and your team members are on the same page about what is needed, you can answer with an appropriate response. By asking questions and clarifying the situation, you can be sure that your response illustrates that you genuinely care about what they are saying, that you are actively listening and that your answers are helpful.

You have learned a lot about essential skills, qualities, and practices you should develop to excel as a leader, but we all make mistakes. Yet, while errors are common, it can be challenging to know how to handle them. Refusing to apologize when you are wrong or apologizing all the time no matter the circumstance is harmful, not only to yourself but to your team. Both a lack of apologizing and an excessive amount of apologizing can reduce your team's trust in you, and therefore hinder the team as if weeds are strangling a flowering plant. When the weeds choke the roots of the plant, it is unable to flower and may even wither, and you don't want this happening to your team. Thankfully, you can learn when to apologize, when not to apologize, and how to apologize.

Let's look at all the basics you need to know to master the apology. First, we will go over when you should apologize and how, before we get into when you shouldn't apologize.

Leaders must understand when an apology is needed. Many high profile business people hire a public relations representative who can help them know when to apologize and when to stand their ground. When a business person truly makes a mistake, an apology is often needed, and you have even seen the CEOs of Facebook and Starbucks, Mark Zuckerberg and Kevin Johnson, apologize for the mistakes they have made or made on their behalf by their employees. Sometimes these apologies are directed at a single person, a team of people, or even to the entire public depending on the situation and who the mistake affected. These apologies are used to mend and repair fractures or broken relationships and strengthen them for the future. When a transgression is left unresolved, it only deepens problems, pulls apart the team, and possibly even ruins a person's public reputation. But, when a sincere apology is made correctly, it can mend the harm that has been done. Once the apology has been made, people can often move on to better things and past the mistakes that were made. Consider, when someone has personally harmed you in some way, you are unable to go about your relationship in the same way as if they did no harm. Resentment will build, as will pain, communication struggles, and more. Yet, if the person makes a sincere apology and accepts it, you two can move past the harm that was done, repair your relationship, and move on to better things. The importance of a sufficient apology done at the right time can not be overstated.

When you realize you have made a mistake that deserves an apology, you shouldn't wait around and allow the wound to fester, as the longer you wait, the more difficult it is to repair. After realizing you need to apologize, make a plan according to the standard rules of apology, as we will discuss in a minute, and then act on it. Remember, some apologies should be private, while others should be public. You will have to consider your specific situation before deciding which is needed in an individual circumstance. There is no need to air your dirty laundry recklessly, but you should sincerely apologize to anyone who may have been harmed by your mistake.

Depending on how large the situation is, you may need to consult with your company's PR representative and discuss possible legal ramifications. If it is a situation that might have legal consequences, you will have to be careful to be transparent without implicating anyone.

When should you apologize? While it would be impossible to create a fully comprehensive list as every relationship and situation is different, there are some standard cases that it is generally accepted that an apology is needed. We will focus mainly on mistakes made on a personal level, in which you will need to apologize to one person or a small group of team members rather than significant mistakes that require a public response.

• You Wrongly Took Credit

When talking about progress and accomplishments with your team or higher-ups in the company, you may accidentally take credit where it isn't due. You may be caught up in the moment and take credit for an accomplishment your team has made, as you are leading the project. However, by taking credit that is due to another, you can create an environment devoid of trust and full of resentment. In this case, you should apologize to the person who you took credit away from and afterward ensure you give them the credit they deserve.

- Favoritism

To lead a team, you need to treat everyone as equal. Sure, there may be some people who have more responsibilities than others, but you shouldn't treat people based on your personal preferences of them. Think about it, if a manager treats one team member better than the rest because they are a relative, then feelings of resentment will form in the team. Everyone will see that you are treating the relative with favoritism, and fractures will develop in your relationships with them. When this happens, you should apologize and ensure you treat everyone with the value they deserve for being a part of the team.

- Harsh Demands

When you're the manager, it can be easy to make harsh demands when there is a lot of pressure placed on you. There is a lot going on, and you want to ensure it gets done correctly and quickly. But, when you make overly harsh demands, it pushes your employees away from you and creates resentment. Anger is no way to lead. You need to be compassionate and patient to develop trust. If you are overly harsh or angry, then you should apologize right away.

- Acting Out of Anger

Again, anger is no way to lead. Whenever you act out of anger or have an outburst, you should apologize to anyone who was affected or witnessed the event. This can happen in many different situations, but it is most common when a team member was unable to meet an expectation and during difficult conversations. Speak calmly, slowly, and focus on communicating without anger. Truly listen to your team members with 360 listening, and even if you don't like what you hear, collect yourself and speak rationally.

- Growing Division

You can accidentally create division in your team if you don't communicate clearly or needlessly exclude parts of the team from projects. Division can happen easily, and if left unaddressed, it will slowly rot away at your team. A good leader needs to recognize when division is happening and when it is due to their actions, apologizing and fixing any of their wrongdoings.

- False Accusations

Nobody is perfect, and when you have to interact with others on a regular basis, this is made clear. When talking with your team members, you may make the mistake of falsely accusing or correcting them when they did nothing wrong. For instance, you may accuse them of not finishing a project on time and correct them, only to realize that you were mistaken about the deadline time and that they did finish on time. When this happens, the mistake should be clearly communicated and apologized for. A large part of avoiding this problem, or fixing it after the fact, is engaging in 360 listening with your team members. We are less likely to listen when we are upset as we want to communicate our displeasure, but this is when we must be the most careful about truly listening attentively so that we avoid mistakes.

- Gossip

Anyone can be guilty of gossip, young or old, male or female, employee or boss. When you engage with gossip, you may think it is harmless, but it causes fractures in relationships. Not only can gossip damage your relationship with the person you are gossiping about, but it can even damage your relationship with the person you are gossiping with. This is because gossip destroys trust and morale. You should always focus on building your team members up rather than tearing them down. If you engaged with gossip with someone, you should apologize to them, letting them know you will refrain from gossip in the future and that you crossed a line. If word got back to the person you gossiped about and they heard what you said, then you should apologize to them, as well.

Now that you understand when you should apologize, it's time to learn how to apologize. The truth is most people do not know how to apologize, and they end up making mistakes that only further harm their relationships rather than mending the fractures. It can be hard to apologize, but there is a precise method that is proven to work when done with sincerity and vulnerability.

When apologizing, you should start by recognizing, stating, and owning up to your mistakes. It is easy to make excuses, but this only pushes the person away. Instead, you should be honest that you made a mistake, the outcome wasn't your intention, but you are responsible and won't place the blame elsewhere. Trying to twist the situation in your favor is the last thing you should do when apologizing. Be completely sincere and honest.

In the same way, you shouldn't make excuses for your actions or mistakes by using the word "but." For instance, don't say "I'm sorry I hurt you, but…." or "I'm sorry I yelled at you, but…" This word is often used to shift blame, and should never be used as such.

While you may want to ask for forgiveness, it is a good idea to avoid this common mistake. This is because when you ask for forgiveness, you are doing it for yourself, to make yourself feel better and ease your conscience. It does not help the individual you are apologizing to, and that's who the apology should be all about. Asking a person to forgive you doesn't even ensure they will forgive you. They may awkwardly say they do, but if it is insincere, then it is meaningless. Yet, if the person truly does forgive you, they will let you know without your prompting. Know that even if the person doesn't feel as if they can forgive you immediately if you are sincere in your apology, they may come around over time. Don't push them, just let them forgive you (or not) in their own time.

Step-by-step a proper apology should consist of:

- Express regret
- Explain where you went wrong
- Acknowledge your responsibility
- Express sincere repentance
- Offer to repair the mistake

Let's look at an example of a good apology following this step-by-step process:

"I am truly sorry that I yelled at you. I was feeling frustrated and overwhelmed and wrongly took it out on you, hurting you in the process. It was my fault, and there is no excuse. I will work to control my anger in the future so that I don't make this mistake again."

While this is a proper apology, keep in mind that there are bad apologies as well. These are frequently referred to as "non-apologies" as the person dresses it up and acts as if they are apologizing, when they are really shifting the blame, making excuses, or avoiding the consequences. To avoid worsening the problem by making a non-apology avoid using phrases such as:

- "I'm sorry that you feel that way."
- This phrase is problematic because it makes it sound like the person is just overly sensitive or thin-skinned, rather than the fault being placed on the person who crossed a line or made a mistake.
- "To anyone who might have been offended..."
- With this phrase, a person weasels out of making a direct and sincere apology to the person or parties that were harmed. It is generic and comes across as insincere.
- "I didn't mean anything by it..."
- By simply saying they didn't mean anything by it, a person attempts to get out of responsibility. They may be saying they are sorry, but then by saying they didn't mean anything by it, they are trying to lessen the consequences of their actions. Instead, you can say, "it wasn't my intention to hurt you, but I did and what I did was wrong." This is better as it allows the person to know your intention wasn't to hurt them, but that you take full responsibility for your actions and mistakes.
- "I'm sorry if I offended anyone."
- Never use the word "if" in this context. The word implies that you either don't know if you hurt anyone or if you did something wrong. It is merely a pretense at an apology, as you are not taking responsibility for your actions, the effect they had, or that you learned anything from your mistake.

Now that you know when and how to apologize, what about when you shouldn't apologize? After discussing the importance of apologizing, it may sound bizarre to say there are times you should hold your ground and refrain from apologizing. Never the less, it is true.

Some people are more prone to apologizing than others. They may apologize for "bothering" others, being late, becoming confused, or they might even apologize for apologizing. It is no wonder that some people become overly dependent on apologizing when they are raised throughout childhood and trained through adulthood to use apologies to deal with a variety of situations. But, if you apologize too much when you really mean it, people will take you less seriously. While admitting when you are wrong, and apologizing shows your strength when you apologize needlessly, it makes you look weak. You will come to resemble a hedgehog that is always trying to protect itself with a defense of "I'm sorry," rather than being equipped to handle difficult situations. Let's look at the circumstances in which you shouldn't apologize.

1. When Asking for the Floor

Do you apologize immediately before speaking up? Maybe when there is a lull in a conversation, and you want to interject something, you say, "sorry, can I add something real quick?" Or, maybe before replying to someone in a meeting, you say, "Excuse me, I would like to reply to what Janice just said."? In any one of these three instances, can you tell me what exactly there is to apologize for or be excused for? You didn't do anything wrong, and you weren't rude.

Some people may even find themselves apologizing when they are rudely interrupted by saying, "Sorry, I wasn't finished with what I was saying." It can be challenging to get your thoughts heard when multiple people wish to speak, but you should never apologize for it. This will only make people believe you are willing to roll over and less deserving of the opportunity to speak your mind. Forgo the apologies in these situations; they do nobody any favors.

Another situation in which you should consider refraining from apologies is when you have to get back to someone. Don't say, "I'm sorry; I'll have to get back to you on that." Instead, let the person know you will get back to their question or statement without apology. In the same way, don't say you're sorry in your voicemail. There is no reason you should be sorry for not being able to pick up the phone, you have better things to be doing, and you can call back shortly.

2. When You're Unsure of Yourself

You might be unaware of it most of the time, but many people will offer a knee-jerk apology when they are unsure of themselves. If they feel they aren't living up to someone's expectations, or that they have failed in some way, they apologize. Even if you run in late to a meeting, don't say, "I'm sorry I'm late," as it only becomes a well-intended distraction. If the meeting is already ongoing, simply sit down in your seat and continue with the meeting as if nothing had happened. At the end of the meeting you can apologize to your boss for being late, but keep the apology short. But, if everyone waited to start the meeting, consider another approach. Instead of being sorry, be thankful. Not only will this let everyone know that they are appreciated, but it will also set you up as someone busy and in high demand. Before getting the meeting going, you can say, "Thank you for waiting, I won't keep us any longer than originally planned. Let's get right to the matters at hand."

3. When You're About to Deliver a Zinger

It's easy to want to apologize when you are about to give someone bad news, but this often only increases the negativity rather than decreasing it. If there was a chance a person might understand your situation, the apology might eat away at their empathy. Worse yet, if you are not to blame for the bad news, by apologizing, the person may place the blame on you regardless. For instance, if you say, "I'm sorry to say, the customer didn't like your pitch," you are apologizing for something that is not your fault. You may hope that the apology will soften the negative news, but in many situations, it backfires without offering any benefit. The apology may even sound false to the recipient, which will increase their feelings of agitation at the unfortunate news.

4. When It's Your Fault

There are times when you shouldn't simply say, "I'm sorry," even when you made a mistake. By offering such a simple and quick apology, you will most likely only anger the recipient, as you don't seem genuinely remorseful. Not only that, but you will also be losing the chance to try to add more positivity to the situation.

One great example of when something is your fault is when your team is not on track to meet a deadline. At the end of the day, if your team is unable to accomplish a task schedule, you are the one who is held accountable, as you are the manager. But, saying, "I'm sorry, I won't have the project done by Wednesday, as we had planned." Try to take the opportunity to give the message in a more positive light, such as, "I know we had hoped to get the project done by Wednesday, and I would really like to finish by then. But, there is an important aspect that I really feel should be included. How about I get it to you by the end of the week so that I can include this aspect?" This response is much more proactive and positive, showing you as a hard worker that makes the best decisions possible for the organization.

As you can see from these situations, there are many circumstances that you can improve communication by not apologizing. Therefore, don't drag yourself down! Instead, they show emotional intelligence, empathy, and quick-thinking.

CHAPTER 3: INVESTING IN YOUR TEAM

When people have been unhappy at work for too long, they look to switch jobs, as the long-term anxiety and health effects of being in a job that costs you your happiness are severe. As a person is stuck in a job that leaves them unhappy, it can cause changes in their weight, blood pressure, headaches, fatigue, and stomach pains. It can even lead people to develop eating disorders, alcoholism, or drug addictions. It is no wonder that all of these problems are more common than ever before, as studies have found that eighty-five percent of people are unhappy with their jobs. Not only does this negatively impact the individual, but it also harms the company. This unhappiness causes nearly 7 trillion dollars across the globe yearly. If an employee is unhappy and chooses to look for employment elsewhere, then finding and hiring a replacement can cost twice their base salary, even more, if they are a high-performer.

Thankfully, you don't have to roll over and simply accept that this unhappiness, poor health, and money and productivity loss is inevitable. While the overall environment and actions of a company affect an employee's happiness with their job, the role the manager has is often equally, if not more, impactful. The manager interacts with their team regularly, and it is up to them to either invest in their team or suck the life out of them. Ultimately, your actions and choices as a manager will determine if your team is satisfied with their job positions. In this chapter, you will learn more about the importance of investing in your team, and more importantly, actionable steps you can take to invest in them and increase employee satisfaction and retention actively.

There are many ways a company can deprive their employees of happiness, thereby doing the opposite of investing in their team. Some ways you can harm employee satisfaction and experience include:

- One of the worst ways that a company can disenfranchise their employees is by poor communication standards. A study found that poor communication can cost a company tens of millions of dollars.

- Micromanaging an employee's every move can stifle productivity, create stress, and reduce employee retention. Nobody likes to feel like their every move is being monitored, even when they aren't doing anything wrong. This is just like how nobody likes to feel like "big brother" (the government) is watching their every move, even if they never do anything illegal.

• Dress codes might have their time and place, but enforcing an unneeded dress code can backfire. Everyone feels more at ease and happier when they are comfortable and how they are dressed plays an important role in comfort. More modern companies are ditching the stifling dress codes, instead of allowing their employees to dress in work casually.

• Lack of extensive employee training can cause an individual to feel as if they aren't developing or adjusting to their new job position. Rather than just having a rule book, detailed training with a manager is an important aspect of employee retention. Employee training is not a negative expense but rather an investment that increases employee satisfaction and productivity.

By avoiding these mistakes, and actively investing in your team of employees, you can greatly improve not only employee retention and happiness but overall business. The truth is, while for far too long the phrase "the customer is always right," has been touted, studies have found that it is more important to prioritize how well you treat your employees. Don't throw your employees under the metaphorical bus simply to please a difficult customer. Famed businessman, Richard Branson, even famously said:

"Customers come second, while employees come first."

By prioritizing how well you treat your employees, you can save your company money by retaining them, build a trusted and solid reputation in the business world, and in the end, improve customer interactions. This is because happy employees will have better interactions with customers, as they know they are valued and trusted. A study found that when happy employees interact with customers, it results in a twenty-percent sale increase over interactions with dissatisfied employees.

One company that is famous for investing in their employees is Google. Not only do they offer the standard health and dental benefits, but they also offer napping rooms, laundry facilities, creative common rooms, free meals, and hybrid car subsidies, they also have policies set in place to promote creativity and free-thinking. For instance, they have a policy that employees can spend up to twenty percent of their time pursuing special projects that they feel is valuable. This policy may, at first glance, sound unproductive to some business people. Still, this innovative policy has led to the creation of many of Google's best products, such as Google Maps, Gmail, Google Talk, Adsense, and Google Cardboard. It is easy to think that only multi-billion dollar companies can be innovative in this way, but even small startups can implement practices and policies similar to these. For example, a small startup from 2013, TargetProcess, implemented the same twenty-percent policy that Google uses, and found it created wonderful results in innovation for the company.

Now that we've examined the importance of investing in your team, it's time to look at actionable steps; you can take to improve their experience, happiness, productivity, and loyalty.

1. Create Individual Development Plans

One of the most straightforward ways to invest in your employees' professional and personal lives is by developing an Individual Development Plan, or IDP. By sitting down with your team members, you can create short-term and long-term goals to help them get to where they want to be. An IDP should consist of a monthly check-in where a manager sits down with each of their members individually to establish goals, track progress, and maintain accountability. You can find many IDP templates online provided by top universities, respected businesses, and even the government. However, you can also create or customize your own IDP plan.

Before creating an IDP with your team members, you should create one for yourself. After all, if you are recommending the benefits of an IDP yet don't use one yourself, it can appear hypocritical. Not only that, but by first creating your own IDP, you can use it as an example as you help your team members create theirs, and you can benefit it to help you reach your own goals, as well.

Most IDP forms will consist of career goals, top strengths, development needs, development goals, and an action plan. Not only should you help your employees fill out this form, but you should also engage in discussion with them. You should allow your employees to lead this discussion so that they feel comfortable coming to you with any of their ideas. Actively practice 360 listening to them during this discussion, asking questions about what they are saying, offering ideas, and helping them tweak and alter the plan so that they can gain the most success. Be sure to offer your own ideas without bulldozing their ideas. During your discussion, there are keys to success you should keep in mind:

- Stay encouraging and sportive.
- Before adding a comment, ask yourself if it is helpful, needed, and worth it.
- Don't insist on all of your ideas or act like a know-it-all.
- Don't make it about yourself, but rather your team members. Avoid talking about yourself as much as feasible.
- Ask for clarification when needed, and don't be vague.
- Don't avoid mentioning development requirements. Sugar-coating doesn't help a person grow.
- Provide feedback, additional ideas, and clarification.
- Offer to help make connections and open

doors.

•   Keep commitments and be available for regular follow-ups as needed.

•   Remember, this is not a performance review; don't treat it like one.

The first aspect you should focus on during the IDP meeting is career goals. After all, the very purpose of this meeting and form is to help an individual develop, but what are they developing for? What is motivating them? In order to make progress, you need first to know why you want to make progress and what you are working toward. As a manager, it is your job to ask your employees about this, to learn if they aspire to another job, a promotion within the company, a lateral move within the company, or if they are content where they are currently at. During this portion of the meeting, you can provide feedback on their goals and offer suggestions or help. The best development plans should address not only a person's current job but also at least two future roles.

After you discuss what a person is working towards, you can detail where they need to develop their skills and strengths while overcoming their weaknesses. Often, this is pulled from a list of generic competencies that you customize to the individual or from a previous performance review. You should allow the employee to assess themselves first, and then you can provide additional feedback. However, don't make this portion of the conversation entirely negative and only about where a person needs to improve. You should also highlight and reinforce their strengths so that they know where they are doing well. If you encourage a person's strengths, they will only continue to grow in these areas, rather than getting discouraged and giving up.

After going over the areas, a person needs to develop and grow; you should set a specific goal for each. For instance, if the person needs to improve their time management skills, listening abilities, or arriving to work on time regularly, you should create a measurable and specific goal so that you can track their progress over time.

Once you have development goals, you need to create actionable steps to improve. It is easy to say you want to improve, but if you actually want to make progress, you first need to create a plan that you can act on. There are a variety of ways a person can take steps to progress, and these will vary based on what their specific goals include. Some examples include taking a course or reading a book on a given subject, finding a coach or mentor, tackling an on-the-job assignment, or moving to a new location.

Lastly, you should tie up the meeting. To do this, you should both agree on the plans that have been made, set a goal date for completion of actionable steps, both commit to the plan by signing copies of the IDP that you can each keep on hand, and set the dates for follow-up meetings on a monthly basis.

2. Begin Full Integration Immediately

When you hire a new member of your team, you need to focus on integrating them into the company immediately. This is not something you can put off. After all, half of the new hires quit their jobs within their first year of employment due to a lack of engagement from management. This means instead of pushing new team members to get to work right away; you should help them become a true part of the team so that they can feel as if they have a place at your company. By focusing on immediate integration rather than instantly putting new employees to work, you can increase employee satisfaction and understanding of their potion while decreasing employee turnover.

Before putting a new employee to work, be sure you:

• Introduce them to the other team members and give them a chance to interact and get to know one another.

• An opportunity to sit down and ask any questions they may have.

• A guideline of the organization's overall mission and how they fit into that mission.

• A clear and easy-to-follow schedule or agenda for their first day and first week.

3. Create Clear Expectations

If you don't clearly communicate your expectations, then your employees will have trouble meeting them. Imagine, if your boss wants you to train a new employee, but they don't communicate this, you will be unable to act on and successfully achieve what they need. The same is true of every member of your team, they need clear expectations communicated on a regular basis. Without this vital communication you may lose good employees, as they will be constantly uncertain. Therefore, communicate expectations both during the hiring process and throughout the person's work on the job.

Each of your team members should have clear expectations of the company's mission and how they are to work towards meeting that mission. For instance, if your organization is trying to make a certain number of sales, then communicate with your team how they can work towards meeting the sales goal. This could be through how they interact with customers, direct sales pitches, or working behind-the-scenes. You should communicate both long-term and short-term expectations with your team. To do this, you first need to understand what your organization's goals are and how your team needs to meet these goals. Once you understand this, you can communicate with your team what you expect them to do on a specific day, on a given week, and for a period of a month.

4. Teamwork Makes the Dream Work

There are several benefits to giving everyone a work buddy. For instance, if they are having a struggle on the job, they can go to their team member for help. This can be especially helpful for when you are integrating new hires, as you can pair them with seasoned team members who can help them adjust to the position. By implementing a buddy system where new hires are paired with seasoned employees, you can also increase the bonds and friendships that they form in the company. This is important, as a study found that the most crucial element for a happy work-life is having friends at the office. However, you shouldn't push team members to be friends, as some people may be able to work together but will simply never be more than coworkers. That is okay. All you have to do is pair your team members up in a buddy system and allow them to find what type of interaction is best for them, whether it stays strictly professional or if they develop a friendship.

You might even find it beneficial to create a buddy system for everyone on the team, not just new hires. To do this, you should pair people up in either pairs of two or mini-teams of four. When pairing people up, it is important that you pair people who work well together. One way you can ensure your team buddies get along is to hear their thoughts on who they should be paired with. Have private meetings with each individual one-on-one, ensuring that nothing they say to you will get out to anyone else. You can then ask each person which people they would most like to be teamed up with and which they don't get along with as well. This shouldn't be about bashing team members they might not care for personally, so instead of asking "who wouldn't you want to be paired with" or "who don't you like" you can ask:

- "Who do you work the best with and enjoy working alongside?"
- "We all have someone we just don't click with, and we have trouble working with them smoothly. Is there anyone you find you wouldn't work well together with on a mini-team?"

By asking in this way you are making it clear that you don't think negatively of any of your team members, you are acknowledging that not clicking with someone isn't a failing, and you are not inviting gossip which should always be avoided.

5. Prioritize Work/Life Balance

Many managers will try to push their teams to come in early and leave late for work. They may even ask their team members to do some work from home, such as answering phone calls or emails during their off-hours. Sure, this may give the company more work without having to pay the employees overtime, but it will backfire. Don't promote short-term benefits that result in long-term disadvantages.

When employees are constantly pushed to promote their work lives over their personal lives, it results in burn out, dissatisfaction, frustration, and unhappiness. Poor work/life balance is frequently the cause for employees quitting and looking for employment elsewhere, which will only cost your company more as they search for replacements and train new recruits. As you can see, the short-term benefits are never worth pushing your employees to prioritize work over their health and personal lives. If you want your employees to be more than staff and a true team that works together and cares about the company, you first have to care about them and their own lives.

Some ways you can promote work/life balance include:

• Restrict hours so that employees rarely work longer than 8-hour days.

• The rare overtime should be paid.

• Don't encourage coming in early or staying late.

• Don't ask employees to work from home without pay.

• When employees take a sick day, trust them, and don't ask for a doctor's note.

• Offer paid telecommuting.

• Encourage paid vacation time and sick leave.

• Ask which religious holidays are important to individual employees, whether it's Christian, Jewish, Muslim, etc. Prioritize giving employees days off for their important holidays.

• Stay flexible.

• Listen to your team members and their needs.

• Trust your team.

6. Celebrate Your Employees

Your team members should not only know that they are appreciated; you should remind them of this frequently. Imagine you are a kid and always helping out around the house, doing dishes, washing laundry, and making beds. You may know that your parents appreciate your cleaning and that it's expected of you, but if they never mention their appreciation, you can begin to feel taken for granted and discouraged. Your employees can feel the same way when they are constantly doing what is asked of them, sometimes going above and beyond, but don't feel as if their effort is appreciated.

One simple way you can let your employees know they are appreciated is to thank them and outright say, "I appreciate it," when they do a good job. Two other great ways are to appoint employees of the month and celebrate their work anniversaries.

When a team member's anniversary of working with you comes up, try writing them a hand-written thank you card and a cake. If your employee has food allergies and is unable to eat cake, you can purchase them a bouquet of flowers instead. You can present them these with your entire team gathered round and give a short speech on why you appreciate them, their accomplishments, and how they benefit the team. This will not only help everyone feel more appreciated, but it will also increase team bonding, further promoting employee retention.

CHAPTER 4: MAKING THE TOUGH DECISIONS

Being a manager requires superior decision making. You are a leader, which is a role that requires you to make hard choices. But, not only are you a leader but having the specific role of manager means you have to handle situations and make decisions that other leadership positions don't require. You might have a vague idea of the different types of decisions that general leaders and managers have to make, but it can be hard to see a clear picture. Frequently people conflate being a leader and being a manager, but it is important to remember that just because you are a leader doesn't mean you are a manager, and therefore there is a difference in general leadership practices and practices for being a good manager. In this chapter, you will learn about the tough decisions managers must make, how you can best make these decisions, and how you can increase your confidence to become a more successful manager.

It takes a lot to be a manager, and all of these requirements can take an emotional and mental toll. You have to work hard to ensure your entire team is satisfied and happy in their position, inspire everyone to do their best, and at the end of the day, you will be held responsible for making the hard decisions. You have to make the tough calls, and any consequences that occur will be on your shoulders. It's no wonder managers frequently become overwhelmed and anxious!

Whether you have just been promoted to the position of manager or have been one for ten years, sooner or later, you will be required to make the difficult choices. This may mean that you have to decide whether or not to fire a team member, who to hire if someone is worthy of promotion, or in some cases, even long-term strategic business decisions. Not only will you have to make these tough decisions on the job, but you will still have to deal with making decisions in your everyday personal life. The pressure from this can become overwhelming, making it difficult to choose anything, even when you know a decision has to be made. You may end up compromising on your choice, allowing others to pressure you, or taking out your frustration on your team.

Decision making is not easy, and the bigger the decision, the more difficult it is. However, as a manager, you must learn how to make decisions without procrastinating, allowing others to pressure you or sway your opinion, or making a quick poor decision just to get it over with and in the past. Instead, a manager must learn to make well-informed, deliberate, and timely decisions despite any difficulties or outward influences. If a manager does not learn how to do this, then they will be unable to excel, and their team will flounder as a result.

Thankfully, you can learn not only to be a good manager but how to make better decisions even when it is tough. You don't have to continue to struggle when instead, you can take action to step closer to your goal of being the ideal manager. It will take time, but if you work to incorporate these steps in your daily decision making, you will find yourself steadily growing closer to where you need to be.

1. Reduce Decision Burn-Out

Studies have found that the more decisions a person makes, the increase in mental burden they experience. Even when these decisions are small, such as what to wear or eat, it accumulates into a decision burn-out that makes it even more difficult to make the tough decisions. While you might not think much of your little day-to-day decision making, it will subconsciously affect you.

The good news is that you can do something about

decision burn-out, therefore lessening your daily stress and making it easier to call the tough shots. One of the ways you can do this is by creating habits as if you form a series of specific habits you no longer have to decide in that situation. For instance, if you have a habit of wearing specific outfits on certain days of the week, you will no longer have to decide what to wear. If you set aside time to create a menu plan for the week, you won't have to decide what to eat on a daily basis. Create a work schedule of the order you complete tasks such as email and phone calls so that you no longer have to decide which tasks to complete first. By creating as many habits in your personal and professional life as possible, you will greatly decrease the decision burn-out.

Another way you can decrease decision burn-out is by having a team that you foster and can trust. If you place your trust in your team, then you can ask them to handle tasks and make minor decisions for you. While you might still have to make the more difficult and important decisions, there are likely many smaller ones that you can leave in the hands of someone you trust.

2. Remove Yourself From the Picture

When we are personally invested in a decision, it becomes more stressful, the New York Times found. This is because we know that we will bear the consequences if the results of our decision are negative. It will personally and professionally affect us. But what can you do about this? It might be easier said than done, but if you close your eyes and imagine that you are not a part of the situation, it can help.

Instead, imagine that some other random person will bare the consequences of the outcome, whether they are good or bad. One way you can do this is to picture how you would advise someone who has to make the same choice. For instance, if you have to decide whether or not to hire someone close your eyes and imagines the advice, you would give a friend or coworker who had to make the same decision. It can help to speak aloud while doing this as if you are actually talking to the person. This will help strengthen your imagination, further distancing you from worry and anxiety. Simply put, we can often more easily see the right answer to a situation when we are not involved, so try to take yourself out of the situation in order to make a decision.

3. Overcome Procrastination: Set Strict Deadlines

One common struggle when making tough decisions is dealing with Parkinson's Law. This theory states that the more time we have to do a task, the longer it will take to complete. For instance, if you know you have to finish writing a report by the end of the workday, you will rush to get it done on time. However, if, on the other hand, you have a full week to complete the report, you will take your time, and likely won't get it turned in until the deadline. While the report may take the same amount of effort in both situations, the more time you have, the more likely you are to procrastinate. This can affect a manager in many aspects of their daily work life, not just decision making.

To help overcome procrastination in decision making, you should give yourself a strict and reasonable deadline. This deadline should be a period of time that you can realistically make a decision or complete a task. If you make the deadline too short, you will push yourself too much, and the quality will suffer in the process, but if you make the deadline too long, you will waste time and procrastinate. The deadline should depend on the specific task or decision that needs to be made so that you can customize it to a fitting time table.

By setting deadlines for decisions, you will ensure you don't keep your employees unsure and nervous while they wait for news on a potential promotion or position change, that you don't waste time when hiring new team members, or frustrate your boss and other higher-ups due to indecision.

4. Limit Your Options

While sometimes we may wish we had more options, the truth is that the more options there are, the more difficult it is to make a choice. Imagine, for many people, when they are surrounded by endless flavors of ice cream, it will be hard to choose the single flavor you will eat, especially if this choice will determine the only flavor of ice cream you ever get the chance to eat. Not only will it be difficult to make a choice when you have to choose between one-hundred flavors rather than three, but you will also be less satisfied with your decision.

When you have a tough choice ahead of you, try to narrow your options to make your decision easier. For example, if you have to choose what candidate to add to your team, narrow your choices down to three options instead of a dozen. Once you narrow down your options, you can then choose between these options with a single determining factor, such as either past experience or enthusiasm.

5. Appraise Your Options

When you don't know what the costs or stakes of a decision are is more difficult to make, as you don't know what the repercussions will be. On the other hand, having a solid list of quantifiable variables, you can easily see what options rank higher than others. Your decision is practically made for you when you see that one option has vastly better variables than the rest.

It can take more effort and time up-front to appraise your options to determine their quantifiable variables, but it is well worth it. For instance, instead of floundering between hiring two possible candidates, you can take some time to go over all the involved variables and to rank them. You might rank their experience, enthusiasm, skills, or cultural fit. Once you have taken the time to quantify all of these aspects, you should have one candidate who is clearly ranked about another, even if only by a single point. This will not only make your decision easier, but it will also give you more confidence in the outcome.

6. Think Long-Term

Often times, when we are worried about the possible negative ramifications of a decision, we think about life in the short-term. You might consider how this decision could affect you, your team, or the company as a whole for the next day, week, month, or even year. Although, you should try to give yourself some perspective by considering the long-term effects instead.

Ask yourself, if you make the wrong decision, how will it affect your life three years from now? Five years? It is likely that if you make a mistake you won't be experiencing any consequences that far down the road. Most mistakes born from poor decisions you will be making as a manager can be resolved in a period of months, or at the longest one to two years for the big mistakes. Therefore, don't put too much pressure on yourself. Don't beat yourself up over mistakes or possible worst-case scenarios. Everything will be okay.

If you follow these six steps, you will find that your ability to make timely and beneficial decisions, even when tough, is improved. Yet, you should not stop there. These steps are only the beginning of the journey; you should also practice improving your self-assurance so that you can have more confidence in your choices. It is especially to foster your self-confidence when you are a manager, as if you want your team to trust in you and faithfully follow your directions, then you need first to trust yourself. If you doubt yourself, then others will doubt you, as well. This can be difficult, as many people have had their confidence in themselves eroded over time due to past mistakes and relationships filled with conflict and mistrust. But, you can regain your surety in yourself with hard work and consistent effort. Over time, you will see that even your team members come to trust you more, as your trust in yourself will be contagious. By empowering yourself, you will, in turn, be empowering your team and the entire company or organization.

But what does a confident manager look like? They are:

• Able to command admiration and respect, even when their decisions aren't popular or liked.

• Willing to nurture people and trust their teams with responsibility.

• Can manage to make decisions for the present while considering the future.

• Able to view situations both broadly and holistically.

• Able to make wise decisions without procrastination.

• Willing to admit when they were wrong, or that someone else's idea might be better.

• Able to remain calm when the going gets

tough.

• Willing to take risks when the rewards outweigh the drawbacks.

Sadly, a person may be lacking these traits when their confidence has been eroded over time or even never existed in the first place. This is often plain to see both by a manager's team members and the higher-ups in the company. Sometimes a manager brings this lack of confidence with them stemming from their personal lives, but other times it is directly caused by on-the-job influences. If a manager feels undervalued or demoralized by their own boss or head manager, it can cause them to lose confidence when making decisions and leading their own team. This loss of confidence may be minor, or in some cases, it can cause a dramatic change in which the manager tried to put off or defer decision making and other responsibilities, as they do not trust their own abilities.

Some managers may feel ill at ease at the realization that there are some people who simply want you to fail. Who is waiting on the sidelines like a vulture for you to make a mistake? They are worried someone will say "I told you so," or take over their role as manager if they fail. It's no surprise that someone in this situation would feel ill at ease, but if you can gain confidence in yourself, you will find that instead of fear and anxiety, you will feel empowered when people look down on you. Many people find this a source of courage, as they strive to prove their detractors wrong

When making decisions for a company, rather than

themselves, some managers might feel increased pressure. This is because they are worried about wasting the company's resources or making a decision that will negatively impact the organization. They are worried about negatively affecting more people than simply themselves. But, it is important that you are not an island; you are working together with a team and the entire organization at your back to support and uplift you.

To build your confidence, you first need to understand why you might lose confidence in yourself. Some reasons might be:

- Focusing on being liked or popular, rather than respected.

- Taking the blame for things that are not your fault.

- Refusing to acknowledge your success.

- You surround yourself with negative people.

- Pursing complete perfection and accepting nothing less.

- Overthinking negative thoughts, creating anxiety, and worry.

- Taking mistakes as a personal failure.

- Comparing yourself to others, thinking you don't measure up.

- Believing you will fail, rather than assuming you will succeed.

- You don't appreciate your unique qualities and skills.

- You indulge in pessimism and listen.

• Dismissing compliments, rather than accepting and appreciating them.

As you can see, there are many ways you might be sabotaging your confidence. If you find that you have trouble making decisions, worry about what others think of you, are increasingly anxious, are reluctant to correct your team member's mistakes, or find going to work a chore, you may be lacking in self-confidence. It is important to recognize this lack of self-confidence, as the first step towards change is acceptance. You can only increase your confidence, and therefore your skills as a manager, if you first accept that you lack self-confidence and then take the steps necessary to strengthen your self-assurance.

Lastly, let's look at some easy and quick steps you can take to gain your own sense of confidence. These can seem embarrassing or needless, but trust me, they will make a difference. Put in the effort to practice them consistently, and you will see a difference.

1. While getting ready for work in the morning stand in a power pose with your hands on your hips, your legs spread apart, your shoulders pushed back, and chin lifted. Next, say aloud one thing you love about yourself. Continue to do this on a daily basis.

2. Think more positively. When you find yourself in a negative thought pattern, stop yourself and replace the negative thoughts with a more positive thought.

3. Don't undervalue yourself, work you regularly appreciate your own experience and abilities throughout the day.

4. Instead of getting depressed by mistakes or setbacks, allow yourself to grow from them. First, identify what you learned from the situation, and then consider how you can decrease the likelihood of repeating your mistake in the future.

5. Learn to express your ideas and opinions confidently, even if you don't feel confident. By speaking with confidence, you will slowly begin to believe in yourself.

6. Put your mistakes behind you and celebrate your success.

As a manager, if you want to benefit your team and organization, you need to prioritize your own growth. You can't help others grow and improve if you yourself are stagnant. But, the good news is that while it does take an effort to grow and be more confident, it doesn't take much time! You can practice steps to increase your confidence through your everyday activities and tasks.

CHAPTER 5: WHEN TO FOLLOW THE RULES, AND WHEN TO BREAK THEM

There are many rules for a manager, which could fill an entire rule book. However, as a manager, you must learn to navigate this metaphorical rule book throughout your daily life on the job, determining which rules should be followed and which should be broken. It can be difficult to know which rules you should religiously follow and which can be left by the wayside, but, in this chapter, you will learn tips and tricks to help you succeed. It may take practice to learn how to develop your ability to determine the helpfulness of specific rules, yet in time you will find that you become an expert.

As children, we were raised to follow the rules, whether those taught to us by our parents, teachers, or society at large. This can make it difficult when we reach adulthood and must learn for ourselves which rules are appropriate and which are not applicable or complete nonsense. It can be scary to go against years of teachings that insist we follow the rules if we want to succeed in life and fit into society. But, the secret is that all the best managers and entrepreneurs know when to follow the rule book as set before them honestly and when to turn away, striking down their own innovative path and creating a better alternative. Some rules are so important that they must be followed all the time, such as those required by law. But, there are rules that are simply lessons taught from the previous generation, which may no longer be helpful or applicable. As a manager, it is your job to be innovative, and know when a rule is either aid or a hindrance.

Many rules are simply passed down from the previous generation and their work experience. The problem is that the world has changed, and the organizations have gone with the flow and changed with the times. If you insist on playing by an old rule book, you will be left in the dust as everyone progresses ahead of you. For instance, while tattoos and piercings used to be taboo in the workplace, many companies now allow their employees to have such things as long as they are well-groomed. In the same way, everyone used to be known as either Mr. or Mrs. [last name] while at the office, but now it is much more common to become increasingly personal and refer to people by their first names unless you have only just been introduced to the person.

Some rules may be inevitably costing the company money, as they create unnecessary steps and red tape. If you can overcome your fear of the unknown and superstition, you can benefit your entire team and organization, becoming a truly great manager and leader in the process. Now, let's get down to the nitty-gritty of rules so that you can learn when to honor them and when to break them apart and break free.

Important Rules to Follow

It's important to keep in mind that while there are many rules you can, and should, break, there are also certain rules that should never be broken. When these important rules are broken, it is a detriment to your team and organization and could lead to your team falling apart or even legal consequences.

1. The Golden Rule

The Golden Rule is a classic; it means you always treat other people in the same way you would be treated. This involves using empathy and placing yourself in their shoes so that you can truly determine the best way to treat them. Simply imagining how you like people to treat you, regardless of the circumstances, is not truly following the Golden Rule. Remember, how people want to be treated depends on their circumstances, so you truly have to use empathy and kindness when you interact with them. For instance, if you are white or able-bodied, you wouldn't mind if someone called you a racist or ableist slur. On the other hand, if you use empathy to place yourself in that person's shoes, you can imagine that these slurs would be harmful. This is how you truly follow the Golden Rule.

2. Safety Rules

There are many different safety rules, depending on your field of work. You might have to stay shaved and wear protective eyewear, or you might have to work in teams when using ladders and place out "wet floor" signs after spills or mopping. Whatever the safety rules for your field of work or organization should always be followed by everyone on the premises.

3. Confidentiality Rules

There are many lines of work that require you to keep the information confidential, whether you are working in the medical field and bound by HIPPA, or have signed a confidentiality contract with clientele. If you break this confidentiality rule, not only will you ruin your organization's reputation and trust, you will likely also face severe legal consequences. This information should only be shared with people who are in the loop, and never anyone outside the office. This means you shouldn't share confidential information with your friends, family, or spouse.

4. Finance Rules

The reason many organizations have rules regarding finances and money isn't to put up red tape or be fussy.

These rules are important, as carelessness can lead to long-lasting and severe consequences. Mistakes in payment, time-keeping, and expenditures could seriously affect the integrity of your organization. You should be meticulous in tracking record-keeping, work times, payment, and expenditures.

5. Business Ethic Rules

Your organization must be completely legal and above board, and therefore you need to ensure that nobody questions your ethical standards and has reservations on working with you. This means you should always be incredibly careful when it comes to sexual harassment in the workplace, a conflict between your team members, potential bigotry, discrimination against disabled candidates and employees, and health safety.

Potential Rules to Break

When considering these rules, you have to take an individual situation into account. Sometimes you can break these rules, but other times it is best to follow them for promising results. Your job as a manager is to determine when to follow the rule book and when to throw it out the window.

1. Big Risks Yield Big Rewards

This popular quote may sound promising, but you have to keep in mind your role as manager. A manager is different from other types of leadership and must be treated as such. An entrepreneur may be able to take a big risk in starting an unprecedented and innovative business strategy, but as a manager, you have a different role. You need to lead your team and support the organization clearly. Many big risks for a manager simply aren't worth it. You have to weigh the pros and cons, and if the drawbacks outweigh the advantages, you shouldn't take the risk in most cases. If you become self-absorbed in taking risks and being innovative, you will be letting your team down. Always remember that your role as a manager is to lead your team, not to create thrills.

2.   Don't Put Off to Tomorrow What You Can do Today

While this rule may sound good in principle, it really depends on the situation. As a manager, it is your job, it analyzes each situation and determines when you should follow this rule, and when you should break it. You will frequently have many tasks that have to be done, and you have to learn which ones to prioritize and which to put off until tomorrow. Sometimes it is important to share heavy information with your team right away, but other times it may be best to put it off until tomorrow after your team has finished completing a specific task.

3.   Jack of All Trades, Master of None

People often act as if a person is failing when they are talented at a wide array of skills, yet have not truly mastered one of them. Yet, the truth is that while some fields may require you to master a given skill (such as jobs in the arts), the best managers are Jacks of all trades. This is because a manager needs to have many skills to allow them to both lead their team and benefit the company. It is more beneficial for a manager to excel in six different skills than master only one while failing at others.

4.   Silence the Rumor Mill

The rumor mill can be incredibly harmful, potentially even resulting in bigotry, discrimination, and bullying. Sadly, you can't actually silence the rumor mill. You may try to stop people from spreading rumors, correct them when you hear them gossiping, but if a person is intent on spreading rumors and gossip, they will simply do it when you aren't around to silence them. Thankfully, there is still something you can do. Instead of silencing the rumor mill, fuel it with the truth. When talking with your coworkers and team members, never spread negative information about each other. Refuse to engage in gossip. Instead, work on actively building up your team to teach others. If you are talking to Jennifer, you can say, "I really admire how hard Carole works," if you are talking to Jeff, say, "Jennifer is a really kindhearted person." If you hear gossip correct it with a more kindhearted and empathetic version of the truth. By doing this, you will be fueling the rumor mill with kindness and truth, rather than unsuccessfully trying to silence it.

5.   Don't Let Them See You Sweating

You need to act strong and trustworthy on the job, that is true. You shouldn't go around the office looking overly stressed and exhausted. Even if you are overwhelmed and tired, you should try to hide these feelings so that your team feels confident about relying on you and coming to you with their problems. However, this doesn't mean that they shouldn't see you break a sweat from working hard. If you are willing to work hard, sometimes even sweating, in front of your team, they will only come to respect you more. They will see that you handled the situation well and aren't afraid of hard work.

6. Trust in Your Gut

It's important to trust your gut, as it often catches unconscious signals that are important to a situation. However, this does not mean we can recklessly make decisions in the name of "trusting our gut." Often times, when a person does this, they are not truly trusting their gut, but rather simply going with their first instinct without truly taking the time to sit down and consider all aspects of a decision. This means when you are making a decision, you should factor your gut into the equation, but don't indiscriminately trust it, especially when you have other information to consider. You will find this is especially important in the hiring process, as while your gut may be telling you something about a person, it could actually be unconscious bigotry against someone who looks different or lives a different lifestyle than yourself.

7. The Customer is Always Right

While many large companies promote the model that the customer is always right or always comes first, this is actually a harmful practice that becomes clear when you work in a smaller organization. Large organizations can often get away with this, as people have little to no option but to work there to provide for their families, and even if they do leave, the company gets so many applications that it won't be long before a person is replaced. But, at the end of the day, this model only breeds negativity, distrust, and toxicity.

You should definitely prioritize your customers and treat them well. However, anyone who has ever worked in customer service or retail can tell you the number of bad customers you will receive. These customers will verbally abuse your team, sometimes even going so far as to hurl bigoted insults and slurs at them. They will make unreasonable demands and refuse to listen to reason. When it comes to these bad customers, they should not come first. Instead, the safety and well-being of your team should take precedence. Nobody should be allowed to treat your team like trash, whether it be a coworker, a client, or a customer. If you treat your team like you would treat your best customer, then your business will only thrive as a result.

8.   Always Play to a Person's Strengths

Like most rules, this one has merit, but there are times it simply must be broken. In general, you want to place your team members on tasks that they are most skilled at and better equipped to handle. For instance, you usually will have your most patient and friendly team member handle customer service while the more gruff and analytical team member works behind the scenes. However, your job as a manager is to nurture your team and help them grow. This is especially true at areas team members aspire to improve in, as discussed during your Individual Development Plan (IDP) meetings. But, they will be unable to grow, improve, and strengthen their skills if you never give them the opportunity. By strategically placing your team members on a task they might be new or weak at, you can help them strengthen their skills, thereby helping them grow and benefiting the company.

9.   Encourage All Ideas and Opinions

A good manager knows the importance of truly listening to their team and valuing their opinions. However, you simply try to listen to all of their opinions and ideas. You could sit around all day talking and not actually getting anything done. Not only that, but some team members might have ideas that are misguided, unhelpful, or directly converse to another team member's ideas. While you should actively promote listening to your team and letting them know that they are free to share their thoughts, there are times you simply have to stop listening. You can do this by saying "okay, I've listened to your ideas, now you get back to work, and I will decide what is best," or "I will think over all of your opinions and let you know what I decide." By stopping the conversation in this way, you are letting your team know that you value their opinion and are truly listening to them, but reminding them that the decision is ultimately yours, and they need to respect that.

10. Treat Everyone the Same

Each and every one of your team members should be valued and treated well. However, this does not mean you should treat everyone in the exact same way. People often promote equality in order to be fair and therefore treat everyone in the same way with the same accommodations. Yet, equality does not allow your entire team to succeed. Instead, you should treat everyone with equity. Unlike equality, when you treat people with equity, you give them each what they need to succeed and flourish, even if it doesn't always look the same. For instance, if some of your team members have a disability or other struggles, they will need to be accommodated differently than your able-bodied team members. They may require tasks that can be accomplished while in a wheelchair, a seat that they can use-as-needed earplugs at loud locations, or earbuds to help them focus on office work if they have ADHD. The goal isn't to treat everyone the same, but to give them all an equal playing field to succeed.

11. Don't Take Sides

It's really nice to say you don't take sides, but this is incredibly idealistic. When it comes to important matters, you simply have to take a stand. This is especially true for managers, as it is your job to make decisions and manage conflicts, which can't be done if you refuse to make or share an opinion.

12. Tell Your Team What to do, How to do it, and

When to do it.

For far too long, employees were constantly controlled and monitored, but this only stifles their growth and potential as if you were hiding a plant away from the sun. Remember Google and innovative startups; they simply provide their employees with the resources and support they need and then step back, trusting them to do the job in the way that works best for the individual. Your team members are not identical robots, and shouldn't be treated as such. If they ask you questions about how or when to do something, answer enthusiastically, but you don't have to control everyone. Sometimes an individual knows how they can complete a task most successfully for their individual traits and skills.

13. Do This, Do That

A surprising number of companies promote actions and rules that are unlawful. Sometimes this is done without an understanding of the law, and other times they hope they can do it quietly and get away with it, despite being illegal. For instance, they may say, "We want to hire someone young so that they fit into our company's culture and look," but this is ageist and will result in a lawsuit. They might not want to hire someone with a wheelchair, crutches, or a service dog, but this breaks the ADA law and again can result in a lawsuit. If your employer asks you to comply with these unlawful rules, bring the issue up with them and make them aware of how it goes against the law, in case they are not aware. And, no matter what, break the rule and refuse to be a part of unlawful discrimination or other unlawful rules your employer may set.

It can be hard to break rules that have been in place for decades or that you have long used. It is okay to examine whether breaking a specific rule is helpful in your situation, and in fact, it should be carefully considered. However, if you come to the conclusion that it is beneficial to break a rule, don't let your preference for the status quo keep you from advancing to a better future. Don't mistakenly believe that just because a rule helped you achieve success in the past that it will continue to serve you in the future.

If you are finding the information in this chapter and book helpful, please consider leaving a review on Amazon so that others may benefit from these innovative tactics at becoming the manager they desire to be.

CHAPTER 6: COMMUNICATION IS KEY

Whenever we interact with others, communication is important. The way you communicate with your boss, clients, and your team will all greatly affect business. As a manager, some of the most important communication you will have to deal with on a daily basis is likely with your team, as to how you communicate with your team affects how clients and customers are treated, how your team gets along, what your team accomplishes, and more.

The Economist released a study titled Communication Barriers in the Modern Workplace, which gives us a more concrete idea of how poor communication skills directly affect your business. This study found that pointless meetings, vague instructions, and other communication missteps can accumulate into larger problems that will severely impact your organization on a wide-spread scale. In this way, it is much like a virus. While the communication problems might start small, they quickly spread until they affect the entire system. The study found that these mistakes can lead to:

- Increased sales – 52%
- Project delay or failure to complete – 44%
- Low morale – 31%
- Missed performance goals – 25%
- Lost sales, sometimes worth hundreds of thousands of dollars – 18%

Let's look at the causes of miscommunication in detail, as if you want to root out the cause of a problem, you first must understand it. Otherwise, you will simply continue to repeat past mistakes. If we again use the Communication Barriers in the Modern Workplace study as an example of what causes miscommunication, we will find three of the causes that they have determined.

Different Communication Styles – 42%

The Communication Barriers in the Modern Workplace study, which we will refer to simply as "the study" in this chapter, determined miscommunication and its root causes by grouping people into generational age groups. This is important, as different generations naturally have different communication styles and habits, and this will have an effect on the workplace. For instance, while only 12% of Baby

Boomers use instant messaging apps on a daily basis at work, 31% of Millennials do, which is quite a jump in numbers.

The problem is that while written messages can certainly go a long way in communicating nuances, this typically involves instant messaging apps that are seen as unprofessional – such as an overabundance of punctuation, emojis, memes, and GIFs. But, since these extra aspects of online communication are seen as unprofessional, and therefore not used on the job, it can lead to a lack of nuance when communicating through writing. Messages can begin to feel colder and leave the person receiving a message unsure about the sender's true feelings. They might fear that someone is passive-aggressive or cold since they are not writing in a more casual personal manner.

On the other hand, when you communicate in person, you are able to better discern the nuances of an individual's intent and feelings, as you can view their body language and hear their vocal cues. This naturally gives fewer opportunities for misunderstandings to appear. A UCLA professor, Dr. Mehrabian, found that 93% of communication is non-verbal, with 38% being vocal (such as tone of voice) and 55% visual (such as body language). This means that only 7% of our communication is verbal, making it plain to see why miscommunications can occur when we communicate through writing, especially in a more professional manner with fewer nuances than we may use in our personal writing.

Of course, this all assumes that a person reads your message. While it is incredibly important to read all work messages, many people will skip reading their email or only skim it for information. Another study found that 60% of people who receive email only read 50% of the message.

Unclear Responsibilities – 34%

When responsibilities are unclear, it naturally causes stress. Imagine, if you know a teacher expects something of you to get a passing grade, but you don't know what, it will cause anxiety; if a relative needs your help, but you don't know what with, you will become frustrated; If your boss expects you to perform well on the job, but doesn't give you any instructions, you might even begin to panic.

The most common place where responsibilities become unclear is at meetings. Another study on the workplace found that senior-level executives spend up to 50% of their time in meetings while managers may spend up to 35% of their time in them. And, the truth is that most of these meetings are unnecessary and unproductive. When this study prodded participants, asking if they left most meetings with a clear understanding of what was needed and what was required of them, a large number gave a discouraging response. To be precise, 46% of the people said they either never, rarely, or only some of the time were clear on what their responsibilities were.

A manager may want to hold regular meetings with

their team to keep everyone on the same page, but this will likely only increase the number of pointless and unproductive meetings. Instead, they should consider communicating with their team members one-on-one in a less formal way. Be sure that what you need is clearly communicated, ask your team members if they have any questions or concerns, and keep things as short as possible.

Time Pressure – 31%

When we have time pressures such as a looming deadline, it results in stress and anxiety, often because we are not equipped with what we need to handle the time constraint. As the deadline approaches, our knowledge of the decreasing time can put us in fight or flight mode as our defenses go up. This causes not only problems for the individual experiencing anxiety, but also anyone who interacts with them in the workplace. The fight or flight mode reduces our brain's rationale, making it more difficult to use the communication skills we have learned throughout life. We may spit out words before we have fully had a chance to consider them, sometimes being unfair or unkind to others in the process. Not only will our words be harsher, but we will also be communicating these feelings through vocal and visual communication.

Whenever there are high-stress levels in the workplace, it is likely a sign that there are major communication problems behind the scenes. It might create a false sense of urgency as if everything on your to-do list is of equal importance when in all likelihood, the importance of items on your list can be ranked. The result is everything begins to feel more rushed, tense, and they can easily become overworked. You can tell the difference between good and poor communication, as while poor communication counter-productively creates anxiety, fear, and tension, good communication instead creates feelings of predictability and stability.

If an employee is stressed all day at the office, they will go home stress and likely spread their anxiety to their family. When morning comes, the person is once again stressed about going into work, meaning the day will start out with people already anxious. The negative feelings in the office will only continue to grow and worsen as it is allowed to continue day by day. The only way to stop this vicious cycle is to stop the root cause and promote positive and helpful communication rather than ineffective communication.

Now that we have explored the three main causes of communication breakdown, let's look at some effects it can have in the workplace, aside from general feelings of apprehension, anxiety, frustration, and fear.

1. Unmet Needs and Expectations

There are many consequences of poor communication that a person might not at first suspect. For instance, it has been found that miscommunications are frequently the cause of missed deadlines, missed appointments and meetings, and people left floundering unsure of what their role on a job should be. When a manager miscommunications something, it affects not only the entire team but often the company as a whole. This is because missing meetings, appointments, and deadlines can reflect badly on the organization and affect client relationships and profits.

If your team is left to figure things out by themselves, they can be confused about the priorities, possibly choosing the wrong task to complete and, in turn, disappointing higher-ups. This doesn't mean that your team members need to be babysat and controlled, but rather that you need to practice communicating your expectations and needs in a way that they can understand.

2. Arguments and Broken Down Relationships

If you have ever been accused by a colleague whether at the office or in your email inbox, you likely understand how much anxiety, frustration, fear, hurt, anger, and helplessness can result from poor communication damaging relationships at the office. For instance, a colleague might appear to accuse you of making mistakes or failing them, rather than asking how a project is coming along or asking questions without accusation.

When you deal with your colleague again in the future, you will likely try to keep interactions short, avoiding them when possible, as the relationship feels uncomfortable and strained. But, oftentimes simply sitting down and having a friendly conversation to find a solution to your problems is the best course of action to take, as doing otherwise only prolongs and worsens the situation.

3. High Employee Turnover

When tensions rise in the company, people begin to dread going into the workplace increasingly day by day. As morale continues to drop, so does productivity, trust, and teamwork. Simply going home at the end of the day feels like a relief, and going back into work in the morning feels like drudgery. People enter a survival mode just to get through the day. As these emotions rise and teamwork goes downhill, it becomes even more difficult to complete tasks and meet deadlines, therefore worsening everyone's emotional states. This is a large vicious cycle that will only continue to grow and storm if you allow it, result in a high employee turnover rate. When your employees leave, you will be forced to spend approximately $15,000 for each new hire to replace them. Not only will you lose out on your previous employees, but you will also be forced to train the new ones with no guarantee that they will stick around. This is because when a new hire comes into a work environment and finds that it is toxic with little teamwork and poor communication, they are unlikely to stay, as it will only be a detriment for them. They will most likely find a new position as soon as possible. If you want to retain your employees, prioritizing good communication and healthy relationships is simply a must.

4. Poor Physical and Mental Health

Studies have long shown that long-term stress results in negative effects on our mental and physical health. It may show as major depression or generalized anxiety disorder, or it may crop up as high blood pressure, migraines, stroke, heart attack, and more. This is why every organization should promote not only health communication and reduced stress on the job but also self-care and healthcare during off-hours, too. By allowing your team to take sick days without pressuring them on if they "really need to," you can ensure your team members stay healthier. This will not only benefit the individual, but it will also benefit the team and company, as if a person puts off their health until it's too late, it will only take longer to recover, meaning even more sick leave.

5. Dissatisfied Clients and Customers

When your team misses deadlines, appointments, meetings, or is confused about what the client needs, it results in frustration and dissatisfaction from clients and customers. This, in turn, will cost your organization their reputation, business, and profits.

Good communication will not just help you and your team members get along better; it will also help you relay information clearly and concisely with fewer mistakes, promote teamwork and camaraderie rather than tension and backbiting, more reliable and consist sales as your customers and clients will be happy to repeat business and more. Some other benefits of good communication include:

1. Fewer conflicts
2. Better relationships with coworkers and clients
3. Employee engagement
4. Increased productivity and talent
5. Innovation
6. Teamwork
7. Transparency
8. Organization growth

Now that we have discussed the importance of good communication in-depth, let's get down to the real task: how do you actually communicate well? Communication takes consistent effort and patience. You can not excel at this skill overnight; you have to practice it with person after person continuously. One important thing to keep in mind is that as we discussed in the previous chapter, there are certain rules that should be broken at times. This means that while there are general practices you should follow for good communication, you may need to tailor your communication to an individual person's needs. For instance, if you notice that a person becomes outwardly stressed when you use specific phrases, you may try using another phrase with this person instead. People who are autistic, mentally ill, or otherwise neurodivergent might require unique communication needs. If you find yourself frequently miscommunicating with a person, then ask them how you can help them. Simply by saying, "I want to learn how to communicate with you better, what can I do to help?" will greatly help a person! Not only will they feel valued and cared for, but they can also tell you plainly what would help so that you don't have to try to figure it out through trial and error.

When communicating, it is important to define your expectations with goals plainly. Remember, as we previously discussed, this is one of the biggest communication roadblocks people experience in the workplace. Therefore, you should consider especially emphasis on this point. You should give clear and achievable goals for each individual person and your team as a whole. Whenever you have a project, you should detail exactly what is needed for each step, to ensure everyone knows what to do and how to do it. Lastly, make sure that everyone involved in a given project understands its objective.

Give your message clearly so that it is understandable and accessible to your specific audience. This means you should speak politely and plainly without beating around the bush or expecting the other person to pick up on subtly. Remember to take into account an individual's communication needs, as we previously discussed. The goal is to communicate in a way that is clear as possible but without causing offense on difficult subjects.

When communicating with a person, choose how you deliver the message carefully. Face-to-face communication is superior in most cases unless the person is neurodivergent and has specifically requested you to communicate through email or other means. Take time to consider whether you should give a message in-person, printed out on paper, or sent through email.

Keep open communication with your entire team. Be sure to ask for their opinion, encourage regular progress reports, and be willing to sit down one-on-one during work hours or lunch break if someone wants to discuss something with you. It is imperative that you make it known to your entire team that they can come to you with anything, no matter what.

Remember that communication is not just about you. It takes two people to communicate, and sometimes additional individuals might even be involved. If you don't fully listen to each of your team members, then communication will breakdown as they realize that you are only listening to yourself. Show them the respect you would desire and fully listen to them, showing empathy and patience.

Lastly, you may create a way for your team members to provide you with anonymous feedback that they may be nervous about giving you. They may be nervous that you might take something personally, because they feel uncomfortable seeking your help for an issue with a coworker, or simply because they suffer from an anxiety disorder. You can easily create this opportunity by having an opinion box and cards that your team members can write something on without giving their names. This will help people feel safe, secure, and still heard.

Remember, communication is key, so you should never neglect this core aspect of managerial skills.

CHAPTER 7: LEADING TEAMS AND INDIVIDUALS

Being a manager is not an easy role, but it is a vital one and fulfilling when done well. Managers are often responsible for engaging, monitoring, recruiting, hiring, training, modeling, motivating, anticipating, coaching, clarifying, evaluating, prioritizing, planning, reporting, directing, adapting, envisioning, disciplining, reinforcing, budgeting, building connections, strengthening relationships, and leading. That would be a lot of anyone to handle, no matter how talented and skilled! This job becomes even more overwhelming when a person feels as if they are at a loss as to how to do their job, how exactly do they lead a team of people? Thankfully, while it may be a lot to handle, you can learn. Within this book, you are provided with the tools you need to succeed, and if you work hard, you will find yourself where you want to be on time.

One aspect you should keep in mind is that while you are managing a team is that every team is made up of individuals and should be treated as such. You should provide guidance for the team as a whole while also interacting with and leading each individual member of your team. There is a very helpful study on group leadership, a key skill for every manager. This study, Exploring the Dual-Level Effects of Transformational Leadership on Followers, examined leadership not only on the group level but on the individual level, as well. This is rare for a study to do, but it greatly helped make the results more clear and helpful.

This study found that when a manager focuses their leadership on each individual member of a team, it created a positive reaction. The individuals in these teams were more likely to perform well at tasks and personal initiative. On the other hand, when a group focused on the whole group rather than the individual members, then the team was more likely to perform well as a group and give each other a helping hand. What does this mean? There are benefits both to seeing your team as a group and as individual members, but you can experience both benefits if you see your team as a group of individual members and treat them as such. If you neglect neither the individual nor the group, you can help your team reach new heights.

If you hope to strengthen your individual members,

then you should coach and mentor them, express confidence in their abilities, set challenging goals, recognize achievements in a timely manner, and allow them to be innovative and creative as they consider possible new ideas and approaches to use on the job. When trying to strengthen your team as a group, you need to practice creating a group identity, shared values, and a shared vision, encourage and promote communication, trust, and cooperation as a team.

On a daily basis, you should consider how you can help your team, both as a group and as individuals. Consider at least one way you can help each individual and two ways you can help the group. By focusing on this every workday, you will ensure that you remember to lead a group of individuals, allowing everyone to prosper and grow. Now that we have discussed the importance of this let's dive into other specific ways you can better lead your team of individuals.

1. Develop Your Emotional Intelligence

Emotional intelligence means that you have the ability to understand and recognize both your own emotions and those belonging to other people. As you can imagine, this is an important skill for anyone, but especially for managers who have to work in a close-knit relationship with a team of individuals. Yet, the importance of this type of intelligence has not always been stressed, leading to many people having a poor relationship with their manager. Consider it, I'm sure you can think of a time before you became a manager that your own manager displayed a lack of emotional intelligence that only made a given situation worse.

Whether you are dealing with your boss or team members, not everybody will be forthcoming when it comes to problems, concerns, or questions. They may be a poor communicator or be intimidated and have anxiety about dealing with their manager. When this happens, people are more likely to keep their thoughts to themselves, even when it would benefit you as the manager to hear these thoughts. This is just one aspect in which emotional intelligence comes in handy. If you have the ability to read between the lines and pick up on a person's non-verbal cues, then you are more likely to help everyone feel comfortable, fully understand the situation, and accomplish a project as intended.

2. Prioritize Understanding

Similar to emotional intelligence, it is important that you work to understand each of your individual team members on a deeper and more personal level. To properly manage your team, you need to understand everyone's experience, skills, weaknesses, motivations, and more. Only by knowing these aspects can you be sure that everyone is working together smoothly and in the most productive manner.

But how can you actually learn these things about your team members? It can seem complicated and daunting, especially when you are starting from square one. Thankfully, the process is easier than it might at first appear, as it mostly requires that you just sit down and have an open and honest conversation with a person.

Directly ask each person what their goals are, what they find motivating, why they are in this line of work, their strengths, weaknesses (don't allow them to weasel out or give non-answers), past experience, how you can most help them if they are having trouble with anything, whether they are extroverted or introverted, and how you can make communication with them easier.

Remember, being a manager requires that you take each person's individual needs into account, and this can only happen if you first get to understand their needs. You should have a preliminary meeting to come to understand them better, and then continue to meet with each person once a month. You can simply combine this meeting with the one for their Individual Development Plan to keep from wasting time.

3. Holistic Check-Ins and Meetings

While you now understand the importance of monthly meetings with your team members, you should also have regular check-ins with those members who hold more responsibility. For instance, if you have members who are heading a given project, you will need to have frequent check-ins with them on how the project is going. During this time, you can discuss workload, progress updates, concerns, questions, and anything else that may be important. Remember always to ask if the other person has any questions or concerns to bring to you.

During your monthly meetings, you should focus not only on your professional relationship with your team members but also personal. You should try to get to know a bit about their lives outside of the office and how they are dealing with life in general. When possible, try to do this outside of the office by taking them to lunch. By doing this, you will put your team members at ease and encourage them to be more personal rather than professional. Try outright telling them to leave work at the office, that you are just going out to lunch as friends. You will be surprised how much of an impact this will make on your team and your communication with them! It will greatly improve your daily interactions.

4. Advocate

As a manager, it is important to remember that your job is not only leadership. You are not just meant to tell your team what to do, how to do it when to do it and enforce that they get it done. No, you are also supposed to be your team's greatest ally. The person that they can trust and go to when the going gets tough. You are meant to encourage and empower them, to reward them for their hard work, to advocate on their behalf.

You should advocate for all of your team members, but especially those who are unlikely to speak up for themselves; Those who would rather roll over and deal with a toxic situation than risk conflict by trying to resolve things.

One way you can advocate for your team members is by relaying their ideas. For instance, if they come to you privately with an idea or a suggestion, but are too introverted to speak up in front of others, then it is your job to advocate for them. If you decide to act on their suggestion, then be sure that you give them credit rather than taking the credit for yourself. You can also take this opportunity to mention to your team that just because a person is quiet or silent during a meeting doesn't mean that they are slacking or putting in any less of an effort than anyone else. That you encourage people to come to you one-on-one when they need or want to.

Another way you may advocate for your team is by going to higher-ups in the company and requesting better care. This might mean you ask for sick days, no questions asked, that your Jewish or Muslim team members get their religious holidays as paid time off, or promotion for someone who has proven themselves.

5. Create an Atmosphere of Safety

The best managers make people feel at ease and safe. When a manager fails at this, it results in team members becoming stressed, frustrated, depressed, and sometimes even fearful. There can be many ways a manager fails to do this, whether it is yelling, punishing people unjustly, being unwilling to listen, allowing bigoted behavior, or even throwing things when angry. Truth be told, there are countless ways a manager can make the workplace space of stress and fear.

A great manager should be willing to stick up for and protect their team, even if it is not in their own best interest. It may make them uncomfortable and nervous, but they are willing to help their team in any way necessary. We have mentioned different ways you can promote an atmosphere of safety throughout this book, but let's round up some of the main reasons:

- You stick up for an individual's best interest.
- You are willing to listen, even to rough topics.
- People are willing to come to you with questions or concerns.
- You don't promote or allow bigotry or discrimination of any kind.
- You don't unjustly punish or get angry.
- You forgive mistakes.
- You are patient and considerate.
- You communicate clearly and openly.

6. Be Willing to Change Your Mind

Everyone is wrong from time to time. Even the smartest and most successful people make mistakes. But, what separates a poor manager from a great one is that they are willing to not only admit when they were wrong but change their course of action based upon their understanding of new information. Pride will only be a manager's downfall, and it will be plainly seen by all those around them. Much like the emperor with no clothes, they will refuse to see their own pride while it is paraded for all to see. It takes great strength to admit your mistakes, and people will only respect you for that strength.

Mistakes could be your choice of how to proceed on a given project on the job, or it could be how you treated one of your team members. If your mistake was how you treated someone, you better be prepared to give a good and honest apology.

7. Promote Team Bonding Time

Sure, a lot of people are reluctant to go to a team bonding activity. However, while everyone often starts out apprehensive, after getting through the awkward beginning, most people begin to have a lot of fun. By the end of the outing, nobody will likely want to go home! But remember, these outings should always count as paid workdays, as you can't expect everyone to come in their precious time off to build teamwork that will only benefit the company.

There are many different types of team bonding you can do. Holiday parties are standard, but you should schedule additional activities throughout the year, as well. Try to at least plan one additional outing per year, though you can always do more if you believe it would be beneficial.

Having a scavenger hunt or going through an escape room is not only fun, but it will also strengthen your group's teamwork. Encourage everyone to share stories, laugh, goof off, and have fun. This will help build bonds and strengthen everyone's empathy with one another.

8. Keep Your Emotions in Check

A good manager must frequently put their emotions on the back-burner in order to prioritize the good of this team. This might mean firing a toxic employee, letting go of someone when business is poor, correcting a team member's repeated mistakes, listening and acting on constructive criticism, mediating conflicts, or taking responsibility with the boss for the team's mistake. While you should listen to your emotions and deal with them appropriately, sometimes there is nothing else you can do but put your personal feelings aside in a given situation. Push yourself past anxiety and discomfort to do the best course of action.

You should especially keep your emotions in check when you are discussing a highly-charged situation. This means that if a situation makes you stressed or mad, you should be especially careful to control your reaction. All too often, people allow their negative emotions to control their choice of words, tone of voice, or body language. When this happens, it only worsens communication, weakens relationships, interferes with productivity, and potentially reduces employee retention.

CONCLUSION

Throughout this book, you learned the skills that are needed for any good manager, and what a manager requires to become truly great. Whether it is resolving conflicts, truly listening to your team, advocating for your team, creating clear and achievable goals, encouraging and motivating team members, leading a team of individuals, or how to empathetically communicate to strengthen your bonds and build your teamwork, you have learned many valuable tools throughout the pages of this book. These tools, when applied consistently, will help you become the great manager you desire to be.

Don't expect yourself to become a great manager overnight. Just as it took time for you to work your way up the ladder and become a manager, it will also take time for you to develop the skills it requires to become great. You shouldn't put an undue burden on yourself to be perfect; we all make mistakes. However, if you learn to grow and improve from these mistakes, you will truly be able to achieve anything.

At the end of the day, remember to treat each person on your team as a person, not simply a cog in a machine of the company. If you do this, building your personal relationship with them and treating them well, then they will come to trust and depend on you. This will naturally lead to better results on the job and a better work environment.

If you enjoyed this book or found it helpful, please consider reviewing it on Amazon so that others may benefit from it, as well! Thank you for reading this book, and I hope you take this opportunity to grow into the best version of yourself truly.

Lightning Source UK Ltd.
Milton Keynes UK
UKHW021823191120
373696UK00003B/479

9 781513 674117